At ✳ Issue

Is the World Heading Toward an Energy Crisis?

Daniel A. Leone, *Book Editor*

Bruce Glassman, *Vice President*
Bonnie Szumski, *Publisher*
Helen Cothran, *Managing Editor*

GREENHAVEN PRESS
An imprint of Thomson Gale, a part of The Thomson Corporation

THOMSON
GALE

Detroit • New York • San Francisco • San Diego • New Haven, Conn.
Waterville, Maine • London • Munich

For more information, contact
Greenhaven Press
27500 Drake Rd.
Farmington Hills, MI 48331-3535
Or you can visit our Internet site at http://www.gale.com

LIBRARY OF CONGRESS CATALOGING-IN-PUBLICATION DATA

Is the world heading toward an energy crisis? / Daniel A. Leone, book editor.
  p. cm. — (At issue)
Includes bibliographical references and index.
ISBN 0-7377-2404-8 (lib. : alk. paper) — ISBN 0-7377-2405-6 (pbk. : alk. paper)
  1. Petroleum industry and trade—Forecasting. 2. Gas industry—Forecasting.
3. Energy industries—Forecasting. 4. Power resources. 5. Energy conservation.
I. Leone, Daniel A., 1969– . II. At issue (San Diego, Calif.)
  HD9560.5.I75 2006
  333.79—dc22   2005046046

Printed in the United States of America

Contents

Introduction

"Civilization as we know it will come to end some time in this century, when the fuel runs out."

—David Goodstein, vice provost and professor of physics at the California Institute of Technology.

Every day, modern nations consume enormous amounts of energy to fuel their mighty economies. The vast majority of this energy comes from nonrenewable fossil fuels, such as oil, natural gas, and coal. Of these fuels, oil is depended on the most, accounting for 40 percent of all energy needs and nearly 90 percent of transportation fuel. Every aspect of modern daily life is dependent on energy. People use energy for heating, cooling, cooking, cleaning, lighting, working, traveling, and entertainment. Industry needs energy to produce and distribute the goods and services on which people depend.

What would happen if these fossil fuels were to unexpectedly decline and deplete in supply? The U.S. oil crisis in 1973 illustrates how dependent modern society is on fossil fuels. Although the shortage was just temporary and artificially created by some Middle Eastern oil-exporting nations, it resulted in nationwide panic and despair, as Americans hoarded gas and feared that their way of life was at risk. Today, if global oil supplies began to decline and eventually became depleted, experts believe the first thing to happen would be runaway oil price increases as supplies constricted. This would result in global hyperinflation, which would permanently cripple economies. Industrial nations desperate for fuel would aggressively pursue control of the remaining oil supplies, which would likely result in war. As Paul Roberts, an energy industry writer, explains, "Competition for remaining oil supplies would intensify, potentially leading to a new kind of political conflict: the energy war." Some predict that an ensuing severe, worldwide depression would force billions of people in war-torn nations to burn coal for heat, cooking, and other basic needs. Experts point out that because coal is the dirtiest of all fuel sources, this move to coal would eventually create irreversible climate damage and an environment unable to support life.

This doomsday scenario is chilling but possible. Scientists claim that these events could come to pass if the world misjudged its supply of fossil fuels and did not allow enough time for alternative sources of energy to be developed and accepted as viable substitutes. Avoiding such a disaster, then, hinges on accurate measurements of fossil fuel supply, particularly oil.

Global oil supply projections vary significantly, however. When considering oil supply, industry forecasters try to predict when supply will peak. Peaking means that oil production has reached its highest level and, unless new reserves are discovered, will begin to decline until supply is depleted. The late Dr. M. King Hubbert, a leading geophysicist of the twentieth century and founder of the peaking measurement model, startled the public with his 1956 prediction of the peaking of U.S. oil production in 1970 and its subsequent decline. He estimated that daily global oil production would peak at 83 million barrels sometime between 2007 and 2010. He then forecasted a sharp decline in production that would bring daily global production to below 5 million barrels by 2100. In contrast, many U.S. government experts project that proven reserves plus undiscovered reserves will support another century of oil production at current levels of use.

How can these huge variations in global oil supply estimates exist? They exist due to the many assumptions that a forecaster uses when preparing an estimate. One of the most significant assumptions estimators must consider is global demand for oil. For example, how will developing nations such as China impact demand for oil over the next forty years as their economies expand? Oil forecasters need to account for this potential surge in demand. Another factor that complicates oil supply analysis is the impact of new technologies on production and exploration. Some in the industry contend that as exploration technology improves, more oil sources will be discovered and developed. As an industry executive in the late 1990s, Vice President Dick Cheney noted the importance of technology in a speech given at the Institute of Petroleum. He stated: "Clearly technology has revolutionized the oil business in the last decade with rapid advances in data interpretation, reservoir management, enhanced oil recovery, directional drilling, and deep water operations, and the pace of advancement is accelerating." However, some experts argue that the impact of technology on oil supply has been exaggerated and therefore should not be weighted heavily in the development of a credible forecast.

Further complications arise from inconsistent data provided by oil-producing nations in the Middle East. Analysts have long feared that many of these states are too corrupt and unstable to accurately forecast their oil output and field reserves. As some of these developing nations fight for a position of power and control in a Western- and Asian-dominated global economy, many political experts believe that these oil regimes have commonly overstated their production capacity and reserves to perpetuate the view that the world is dependent on Middle Eastern oil.

While experts debate how long global fossil fuel supplies will last, it is apparent that alternative sources of energy will eventually need to be developed. Many contend, in fact, that the development of these alternative sources needs to be accelerated to ensure a smooth transition. They argue that a global energy crisis will begin when worldwide oil production begins to drop, not when it is depleted. According to David Goodstein, "The crisis will come not when we pump the last drop of oil, but rather when the rate at which oil can be pumped out of the ground starts to diminish." As most experts believe it will take decades to develop and achieve societal adoption of alternative sources of energy, many feel that the energy industry and governments need to adopt a greater sense of urgency and should be accelerating alternative energy research and development.

Others discount the need for immediate government action, contending that natural economic market forces will dictate a smooth transition to alternative energy when necessary. They purport that as fossil fuel becomes more scarce and expensive to produce, alternative sources will be developed and offered as economically competitive substitutes. Furthermore, they argue that this process has already begun as the energy industry anticipates fossil fuel shortages and is exploring new opportunities in alternative energy production.

Energy will be a critical issue in the twenty-first century, as fossil fuels become more scarce and new energy sources are developed. While some believe that fossil fuel supplies will last through the century, allowing sufficient time to develop new energy sources, others contend that a catastrophic world energy crisis is on the horizon and will trigger the end of modern civilization. Authors in *At Issue: Is the World Heading Toward an Energy Crisis?* explore and debate the amount of fossil fuels the world has left as well as solutions to energy shortages such as energy conservation and alternative energy sources.

1

The World Is Running Out of Oil

Matthew Simmons

Matthew Simmons has been a key adviser to the Bush administration's 2001 Energy Task Force. He is also an energy investment banker and is CEO of Simmons and Co. International, an investment bank specializing in the energy industry.

There is a strong possibility that the current world oil supply is peaking. Further growth in the oil supply will end, and a relatively quick transition will begin toward a steady and serious decline. If oil is peaking then it is likely that natural gas will quickly follow, as its supply will be used to cover oil shortages. Unfortunately, the current methodology for estimating world oil supply and demand is imprecise. As a result, it is likely that peaking and the subsequent decline in world oil production will be identified only after it has begun. This failure to act in a timely way will cause a catastrophic global energy crisis, and there is currently no plan to avoid it.

Editor's note: The following viewpoint was originally given as a speech at the second international conference of the Association for the Study of Peak Oil on May 27, 2003.

E nergy . . . might turn out actually to be one of the most important topics for the well being of the globe over the next fifty years. [The question] basically (is), "Is the energy glass half full or half empty?" So let me . . . just share some of the issues that I think are important.

First of all, the topic of whether the energy glass is half full or half empty is right. It basically elicits some of these talks from so many people that start out with positions saying, "The glass is half empty, we will never run dry."

But the real issue . . . , basically speaking, does not . . . mean running dry. The debate on how long the dwindling of supplies might take has been extremely controversial. In fact, I'd say that most of the debate has been one-sided.

> **//** *All great crises were ignored until it became too late to do anything about [them].* **//**

Optimists argue that the issue is still years away, and to their support, . . . it has never happened before and [yet has] often been predicted. And each time the future looks bleak, the optimists argue, it's always darkest before dawn. It is also interesting how many people basically look at undiscovered reserves and say that we really don't know how much we still have left to find. . . . [But] there's no guarantee that the reserves are actually there.

I come back to the basics and say I think that one thing that we . . . all know is that oil and gas resources are genuinely nonrenewable and so someday they will basically run out. And also, we are using 28 billion barrels a year; that's a lot of energy to be consuming. And peaking, as you all know, is different than running out. Is "peaking" an important question or issue?

First of all, if you start out by saying usable energy is the world's most critical resource then obviously it is an important issue. Without volume energy we have no sustainable water, we have no sustainable food, we now have no sustainable healthcare. And since five-sixths of the world still barely uses any energy it really is an important issue. And since five-sixths of the world is still growing fast or too fast it's even a more important issue.

What peaking does mean, in energy terms, is that once you've peaked, further growth in supply, is over. Peaking is generally, also, a relatively quick transition to a relatively serious decline at least on a basin by basin basis. . . .

Peaking of oil is also probably then assuming peaking of gas too. So is this issue important? I think the answer is an emphatic yes. Why does this issue evoke such controversy? Well, I think for several reasons; first of all the term "peaking," unfortunately, does suggest a bleak future. It also suggests high future energy prices, and neither are pleasant thoughts.

I think it is human nature . . . to say that we really like to have pleasant thoughts. And crying wolf is bad business unless the wolf turns out to be already at the front door, and by then, the cry is generally too late. And crises are basically problems, by definition, that got ignored. And all great crises were ignored until it became too late to do anything about [them]. And so if the issue is serious, why are the answers so dissenting? I think the reasons are several-fold. First of all, the data and the methodology to estimate total energy resources is still remarkably hazy, and [it] takes a lot of fuzzy logic to get to the bottom line.

Judging the data, for instance, on current decline rates on even fields per basin is very hard to define. And it turns out that peaking is one of these fuzzy events that you only know clearly when you see it through a rear view mirror, and by then an alternate resolution is generally too late.

The Voice of the Energy Industry

Over the course of the last few years, conventional wisdom in the energy business became "do not trust conventional wisdom." The voice of energy, for better or worse turns out to be the International Association of Energy Economists [IAEE]. . . .

This group basically had a mantra throughout the decade of the nineties that growth in energy demand is suspect, that energy supplies are surging, that Moore's Law has brought down semiconductors at a cost so dramatically it will bring energy prices considerably lower, that OPEC [Organization of Petroleum Exporting Countries] is obsolete, and a non-sustainable concept.

[Some time ago], the IAEE had their 25th annual meeting in Aberdeen, and I attended the program. It was really interesting. On Saturday morning, they had 13 of the past 25 presidents talking for the better part of two hours, and individually reflecting on the lessons that they had learned over the past 25 years. . . . What I heard most, was the word, "conventional wisdom." This was the big mistake I personally made 25 years ago. Twenty-five years ago, I thought demand was going to go up fast and that was wrong, I thought that oil prices were going to 100 [dollars per barrel], and that was wrong, and I thought the OPEC was omnipotent, and that was wrong, and I thought that supplies basically were going to be a pot of gold and that was wrong, and what I learned personally is to never trust "conventional wisdom." And by the time all thirteen speakers had spoken, it was clear that their belief had become conventional wisdom. It turned out that basically the generals, as happens so often in the military, were fighting the last war. The big energy mistake[s] that were made, circa 1980–1981, was that oil was going to go to 100, that the demand growth was insatiable, and that OPEC was omnipotent. And what all these people missed at the time was that the oil prices had already grown tenfold; that nuclear energy was at the front door, that the fear of a hundred dollar oil had finally created a conservational efficiency move and that a ten-year E.P. [environmental protection] movement created a surplus glut. And preventing . . . this mistake again became public enemy number one and literally led a generation of energy experts to mistrust demand, to assume supply growth and . . . to know that price collapse was just around . . . the corner.

But it is interesting now with the benefits of being in a new millennium, to look back and see what really happened to oil demand over the last 30 years. First of all, global oil demand did fall in 1974 and halfway through 1975. But over the course of the first eight years of the 1970's, global oil demand grew significantly. Global oil demand then fell in 1979 through 1983. And so you had five of thirteen years down but the two events that caused this down demand were a tenfold increase in product and the introduction of the only new energy source native to the 20th century: nuclear. Global oil demand began to grow again in 1983. The collapse of the F.S.U. [former Soviet Union] from 1988 to 1995 created the illusion of global stagnation while the rest of the world's oil demand and energy just grew and grew and grew.

And it's interesting to step back and look at the difference between 1986 when non-FSU oil demand was just under 54 million barrels a day, to 2002, when we crossed 73 million barrels a day . . . a 21 million barrel a day change during an era [when] people thought . . . that demand growth was over.

World Oil Supply

And then let's turn briefly to what happened to the world's supply. Well, first the former Soviet Union supply collapsed. Secondly, the North Sea had its second boom. Third, deep water became the new frontier and probably the last frontier, and fourth, OPEC remained the swing producer. If you . . . look at the non-OPEC numbers excluding the former Soviet Union, you basically have a growth between 1986 and 2002 of 8.3 million barrels a day. Now it's interesting to see that global oil growth and demand was 20 and non-OPEC, non-FSU growth was 8.3. But if you look carefully at the 8.3, in the first ten years, 1986 thru 1996, during an era of low oil prices, we grew by 6.7 million barrels a day, and in the last six years, during the era of high oil prices, we grew by 1.5 million barrels a day. So 81% of the last fifteen years' growth . . . came during the era of low prices, and 19% came during the era of high prices. It turns out with just hindsight that we can now clearly see that the growth engine of non-OPEC oil, excluding the former Soviet Union, petered out. The North Sea peaked, Latin America excluding Brazil peaked, North America, excluding heavy oil peaked, Africa excluding deep water peaked, the Middle East excluding OPEC peaked, and the F.S.U. turned out to be the only lasting pleasant surprise.

> *There has been no significant FSU [former Soviet Union] exploration yet.*

Which then raises the following question: Was the F.S.U. recovery real and sustainable? In 1998–1999 not a single oil expert assumed that the F.S.U. would suddenly turn around and start creating supplies again. But then low oil prices created through the saga of the missing barrels caused the ruble to collapse. And subsequently high oil prices created an F.S.U. bonanza, low global prices and unbelievably high revenues. 67% of the 2000–2003 non-OPEC supply came with the F.S.U.'s oil recovery. Some of this increase was unlikely due to bad data and some of the increase was a one time gain.

There has been no significant FSU exploration yet. It's simply too expensive. And logistical bottlenecks create some significant limits to further export growth. So I think it's dangerous to assume that the FSU growth will continue. In the meantime the cost to create new oil supply soared.

While conventional wisdom believes where there's a will there's a supply, real costs to maintaining flattening supplies soared. Between 1996 and 1999, the 145 Public E&P [Energy and Petroleum] companies . . . worldwide spent 410 billion dollars to merely keep their full production flat at about 30 million barrels of oil per day. The Big Five, Exxon, Shell, BP [British Petroleum], ChevronTexaco, and Total spent 150 billion dollars between 1999 and 2002 to barely grow production from 16 billion barrels of oil a day to about 16.6.

The Big Four, excluding Total, between the first quarter of 2002 and the first quarter of 2003 went from 14 million, 611 thousand barrels of oil equivalent per day to 14 billion, 544. These four companies spent collectively over 40 billion dollars over a 12 month period of time [and] actually lost 67 thousand barrels a day of total production. So while people were assuming costs would fall, the cost to stay in the game went through the roof.

Eliminating Dry Holes

One of the other interesting mantras of the last decade was that technology had eliminated dry holes. Well we never came close to obsoleting the dry hole. The reason dry holes dropped so much is we drill far less wells. We also stopped doing most genuine exploration. Even projects that are called wildcats today were called modest step-outs 20 years ago. It turns out that now that we look back with good data . . . it is still a risky business. . . . The Caspian Sea, other than one great discovery, has been bad. And even the Middle East is starting to dig a remarkable string of dry holes. . . .

> *When giant [oil] fields do peak they basically also do decline.*

The reason supply flattened out or peaked was not lack of effort but rather from a lack of new technology. The industry in fact had many great successes over the last decade. But they were not about to offset depletion. Smaller new fields were found, technology allowed them to be commercial, but we raised the climb rate to an amazing level. [As a result, supply] began to flatten out.

Why is oil depletion so hard to grasp? Well the definition

by itself is hard. Many would hear the term depletion and assume it meant that we ran out, and we obviously never ran out of oil. Depletion data was sketchy at best. It's amazing how hard it is to actually dig out statistics for, even on a field by field basis, what the net decline is. And the elusive data that you can find is not real depletion, . . . it's actually the net decline after lots of additional drilling and money is spent to take a natural decline rate that would have been far more drastic if you flattened [it] out. . . . No one really likes to discuss it much because it should generally mean bad news.

Forecasting Oil Supply Is Difficult

Forecasting next year's decline still remains an art form. I don't think anyone has ever been very good at predicting bad news. There are many ways also to slow natural decline, but it takes money and effort, and it's only when you look back, after these remediation efforts have been done, that it creates real depletion answers. But let me tell you that as you all know, wells, fields and basins really do deplete. Our firm . . . conducted a very intensive analysis of what was happening to the natural gas supply in Texas by examining the detailed records of the Texas Drill Commission from 50% of the state's production in 53 counties. What we found was amazing. We found that in this 53 county area (this is 16% of the U.S. gas supply) of the wells drilled in 2001, 2,400 wells out of 37,000 wells that are in production created 30% of the total supply. It turns out that 7% of these 2,400 wells, 167 wells, created 49% of the supply, and the other 93% of the wells created the remaining 51%. . . . A year later, we went back and tested [the giant wells'] January 2003 production; they had suffered a decline across the board of an average of 82% in a year, so wells do decline rapidly these days. The Cruz Beana field in Colombia, the biggest find in the Western Hemisphere since Prudhoe Bay, in 1991–1992 . . . was still estimated that it could possibly exceed Prudhoe Bay or Hatchet. But it turns out that this field . . . just barely gets 500,000 barrels a day. And in 2002 it's struggling to stay above 200,000 barrels a day. The Forty Field, which BP just recently sold to Apache, peaked at approximately 500,000 barrels a day in the middle eighties and the oil production is now under 50,000 barrels a day. It still produces about 500,000 barrels a day of fluid, but the balance is processed water.

And then you finally have the . . . last two Super Giant

fields ever found. Ironically these two fields, Prudhoe Bay and Samotlor, were both found in about the same crust underneath the Arctic Ocean. They were just found on two sides of the earth. Both were basically found within twelve months of one another, 1968 and 1967, both were presumed to have 15 to 20 billion barrels of oil. It's interesting to see that Prudhoe Bay's reservoir management . . . basically choked off the field at 1.5 million barrels a day. . . . For over 11 and almost 12 years, like clockwork, it produced 1.5 million barrels a day without missing a beat. But in late 1989 the field rolled over and is now producing about 350,000 barrels a day. Samotlor [Russia] had just the opposite experience. They basically started aggressively water-flooding a very wide field and it produced peak production at about three and a half million barrels a day. . . . Then it came off like a waterfall and is again down to 325,000 to 350,000 barrels a day. And so when giant fields do peak they basically also do decline. There's no question that when you take 50% of a remaining resource you tend to alter peak. What is difficult though is to obtain the right data to know whether you've reached 50%. And it's basically that you're looking back through events with hindsight. It turns out that total energy resources . . . [are] still a mystery. And recoverable percentage of resources is also largely a function of cost. The higher the cost the more you can extend, recovering more and more of the harder and harder to get resources.

Little Change in Gauge Technology

And it's also interesting when I think back on this that the technology to gauge resources, absent of seismic, is still effectively 100 years old. We have no better technology today to know how much resources are there before seismic is done than we had 100 years ago. And even after a few of them test their research you still leave many questions, and so it's based on opinions. Let me give you some interesting examples of the [uncertainty] of this data. I attended a Natural Gas Workshop in Washington, D.C. . . . and the head of the U.S.G.S. [U.S. Geological Survey] made an interesting presentation about how hard it is to basically get experts all on the same page even when you have a complete set of data. One of his examples was the . . . basin in Argentina.

Two hundred and nineteen mature fields. They had a data set that allowed all of the experts to basically use any one of the

7 conventional methodologies to say how much remaining resources are there. And after a weekend of study the estimates came back with a low of 600 million barrels to recover to a high of 17 billion barrels. This is on a mature field area with 219 individual fields. Canada's recent experience in Sable Island is a classic example of how little you sometimes know even after the fields have been in mature stages of production. It turns out that Sable Island looked like a fabulous project through wells one through five, and then well six was drilled and they found basically it was little, they miscalculated the amount of reserves, and so 37% of the proven reserves of Sable Island in the last few months were written off. The Leaden Field, which is the largest project in U.K. sector of the North Sea last year [2002]—six months into its production the company had new data that basically highlighted the reserves, the reservoir's complexity so that half the reserves were transferred from proven into probable.

> *" Hindsight turns out to be a wonderful, unreliable tool. "*

And then another interesting presentation in the natural gas workshop in Washington was on center basin gas, which . . . pipes gas in the Green River basin, where some new evidence would indicate that we've overstated potential recoverable reserves by three to five times.

All of which highlights how difficult it is to basically get your hands around how much is left until you're looking back at events with hindsight. Hindsight turns out to be a wonderful, unreliable tool. Some events are unpredictable until after the fact. Some of the classic unpredictable events turn out to be weather, death, one's peak net worth, and maybe the future of anything important. It turns out that peaking even for an individual well is only proven after the fact. And predicting peaking of energy has been an elusive art form for a long period of time. So back to the United States of America and our experiences in oil as a classic example of how hard it is to predict peaks. In 1956 Dr. [M. King] Hubbert predicted in the early seventies . . . [that] the United States would peak. In 1970 it was obvious he was wrong when the U.S. set a new record, the new

U.S. peak. In 1981, what had been 9.6 million barrels by, at its peak, was already down to 6.9 million barrels a day after a record drilling boom. And by 2003 this 9.6 billion barrel basin in 1970 is now close to 3 million barrels a day. The U.S. was Saudi Arabia in 1956. We had great statistics, we had total transparency and yet only one person predicted the peaking in 1970. Did the United States get a lot smarter? Well the U.S. Natural Gas experience is a great new case study.

Natural Gas Supply

In 1999 the Natural Petroleum Council projected that supply growth in natural gas would be adequate to increase gas use by 36% by 2010. In 2001 we had a record drilling boom for natural gas. This failed to budge supply. In 2003 natural gas clearly faces a crisis. [Production in] the United States and Canada is in decline.

What we all missed in 1999 was that no one could come to subtract unconventional supply growth, coal bed methanes, tar sands, deep water associated gas, and these giant gas wells down to 18 to 20 thousand feet vertical, from the conventional base: [we] discovered conventional base at about fifty feet . . . [p]eaked through Europe in the nineties and is now approximately 35 BCF (Billions of Cubic Feet) a day. So it turns out the United States . . . has experienced about the same phenomena that oil did 30 years ago.

Serious energy planners need to assume non-OPEC supply is at a plateau.

The North Sea experience is interesting. The North Sea had all the world's best operators, state of the art technology. Its peak was assumed to be years away in 1996 and 1997. In 1999 the U.K. Sector peaked. In 2002 the New Eastern sector peaked. The North Sea has the world's best field by field production data. Seeing peaking is easier in the North Sea than anywhere else but few people seem to study the data. Peaking, it turns out, even in the North Sea is easy to ignore. And then there's the experience of the Caspian Sea.

In the early nineties the Caspian seemed to be the next

Middle East. In 2001 we had 20 out of 25 dry holes that dampened the enthusiasm for the Caspian significantly. In 2001 Kashagan was finally discovered, deemed to be the greatest field in the decade. In 2002 BP and Stat Oil quietly sold their 14% of Kashagan for 800 million dollars. In 2003 British Gas put their 17% on the block for 1.2 billion dollars. Which raises, in my opinion, the question, "What do these original parties know about the world's greatest field or do they merely want to spread the wealth? I think what this all means is that non-OPEC oil, particularly outside the Soviet Union, is either peaking as we speak, or has already peaked.

Non-OPEC Oil Peaking

Any serious analysis now shows solid evidence that the non-F.S.U., non-OPEC oil has certainly petered out and has probably peaked. F.S.U.'s supply is suspect or should be. A new frontier is always a possibility but it is becoming increasingly unlikely. . . .

And serious energy planners need to assume non-OPEC supply *is* at a plateau. But thank heavens for the Middle East. The big non–Middle East OPEC producers are also past the peak. Algeria and Libya could probably still grow but they're too small to offset everyone else. And only the Middle East can logically be explained to replace declines elsewhere.

The Middle East: The Promised Land

The Middle East's transparency is an oxymoron but there are some data that shed some light. And so let's . . . spend a few minutes looking at the Middle East, the Promised Land.

Middle East energy is the Promised Land. All roads . . . lead to Rome, and to the future of oil and gas, Rome is the Middle East.

The Middle East is where we still have abundant reserves. It's still cheap to produce; it's still extremely unexplored. So if the rest of the world is long in the tooth, thank Allah for Mecca. But are we so sure this is the truth? It turns out that the Middle East oil and gas so far is *not* all over the Middle East. The Middle East covers an enormous land mass, but all of the oil and gas as we know it today is compressed into an interesting golden triangle. And all the great finds happened years ago. In the past three decades exploration success has been modest in the Middle East abyss. Is this because no one looked very hard or because there's not much else to find? Here is the interesting golden triangle of the Middle East; if you start at Kirkuk in the north and you draw a line down through the great oil fields of Iran, going down south and come over six or seven hundred miles picking up the great fields of the UAE [United Arab Emirates] and come back up 800 miles to Kirkuk, virtually every field of any size between 1909 and the late sixties is probably in that basin.

It turns out that Saudi Arabia has what they thought was a fabulous discovery outside that in 1989. By 2003 one field . . . needed gas injected to create flows to get about 200,000 barrels a day. So it's also interesting to take the United States and superimpose this same golden triangle on part of the United States . . . I grew up in. It basically covers most of Arizona and part of Utah, so it's *not* a very big area. So if all roads lead to Rome then one area, Saudi Arabia, is clearly home port. Saudi Arabia became the most important oil exporter once the U.S. peaked. Though also not trusted, Saudi Arabia has constantly tried to become the world's most trusted supplier of oil and they generally have done that. Saudi Arabia has assumed a virtually limitless amount of cheap oil. But let me tell you about some of Saudi Arabia's oil and gas challenges. In Saudi Arabia there have been no major exploration successes since the late sixties. Almost all of Saudi's production comes from a handful of very old fields. Almost every field has high and rising water pressure. Ghawar, the world's largest field, injects seven million barrels a day of seawater to prop up reservoir pressure. . . . Some key fields have never worked out. Others have now watered out. And it takes utter logic to plan for Saudi Arabia's future.

What Saudi Arabia's real energy costs might be is that Saudi Arabia is probably no longer a low cost producer. Lifting costs, plus, may now rise exponentially. Natural gas parting costs are extremely high and have been elusive. But what is Saudi Arabia's right price for oil? I would argue that no one really knows because we lack the data.

The Optimists and Pessimists

But it turns out with a little bit of hindsight that the optimists turned out to be wrong. While the optimists estimate, the economist rectifies, the debate still rages on; the jury basically has now rendered the verdict. The optimists have lost. Too much field data now proves their total thesis was wrong. Supply never surged, demand did grow. But as it grows it still falls. This doesn't prove though that the pessimists were right. The pessimists unfortunately and ironically might also be wrong. Most serious scientists worry that the world will peak in oil supply. But most assume that this day of reckoning is still years away. Many also assume that non-conventional oil will carry us through several additional decades. They were right to ring the alarm bell. But they too might also be too optimistic. Non-conventional oil unfortunately is too non-conventional. Light oil is easy to produce and convert into usable energy. Heavy oil is hard to produce and extremely energy intensive and very hard to grow rapidly. It turns out the United States of America has nine fields left that still produce over 100,000 barrels a day. And three of the nine have turned out to be located in California and on average are 103 years old. The reason these fields are still there is that they're very heavy oil. And heavy oil can last forever, but it's very hard to get out of the ground. And it takes a remarkable amount of energy to convert heavy oil into usable energy.

The facts are too serious to ignore.

Five years ago I barely had thought about the question of, "What does peaking mean and when might it occur?" I was intending at the time . . . to study the concept of depletion and the phenomenon that field after field was tending to peak fast and decline at rates that were unheard of before. . . . I think now that peaking of oil will never be accurately predicted until after the fact. But the event will occur. And my analysis is leaning me more by the month to worry that peaking is at hand; not years away. If it turns out I'm wrong, then I'm wrong. But if I'm right, the unforeseen consequences are devastating.

No Backup Plan

But unfortunately the world has no Plan B if I'm right. The facts are too serious to ignore. Sadly the pessimist-optimist debate started too late. The Club of Rome humanists were right to raise the "Limits to Growth" issues in the late 1960's. When they raised these issues they were actually talking about a time frame of 2050 to 2070. Then time was on the side of preparing Plan B. They, like Dr. Hubbert, got to be seen as Chicken Little or the Boy Who Cried Wolf. . . .

In 1957 the [Soviet] Sputnik woke up the rest of the world. By 1969 [the United States] had a man on the moon. That was not easy, but the job got done. Could an energy Sputnik create a similar wake-up call? If we had such a wake-up call is it too late? Is there . . . an Apollo program that would work? It turns out that reliable energy is the world's number one issue. Creating reliable and affordable energy opens the door to solving the problem of the world's water, food, and healthcare. Without reliable energy all these other needs dull.

The world is still growing. There [are] five billion people on the earth today that are still either maturing in age or yet to be that old. And five billion people still use little or no energy. If the world's oil supply does peak, the world's issues start to look very different. Thank heaven the debate began even if it might have been too late.

2

The World Is Not Running Out of Oil

David Deming

David Deming is a professor at the University of Oklahoma's School of Geology and Geophysics and is an adjunct scholar with the National Center for Policy Analysis, a nonprofit public policy research institute seeking private sector solutions to public policy problems.

Over the past century scientists have often predicted that oil resources would run out within a few years. Despite these dire predictions, global oil production has continued to increase through the end of the twentieth century. New technologies have allowed for greater oil recovery than ever before, and higher market prices have financed further exploration. As technological advancement continues, new oil sources will be discovered and developed. The world will eventually run out of oil but not until at least 2100.

O il is a nonrenewable resource. Every gallon of petroleum burned today is unavailable for use by future generations. Over the past 150 years, geologists and other scientists often have predicted that our oil reserves would run dry within a few years. When oil prices rise for an extended period, the news media fill with dire warnings that a crisis is upon us. Environmentalists argue that governments must develop new energy technologies that do not rely on fossil fuels. The facts contradict these harbingers of doom:

- World oil production continued to increase through the end of the 20th century.

David Deming, "Are We Running Out of Oil?" *Policy Backgrounder*, no.159, January 29, 2003. Copyright © 2003 by the National Center for Policy Analysis. All rights reserved. Reproduced by permission.

- Prices of gasoline and other petroleum products, adjusted for inflation, are lower than they have been for most of the last 150 years.
- Estimates of the world's total endowment of oil have increased faster than oil has been taken from the ground.

How is this possible? We have not run out of oil because new technologies increase the amount of recoverable oil, and market prices—which signal scarcity—encourage new exploration and development. Rather than ending, the Oil Age has barely begun.

The History of Oil Predictions

The history of the petroleum industry is punctuated by periodic claims that the supply will be exhausted, followed by the discovery of new oil fields and the development of technologies for recovering additional supplies. For instance:

- Before the first U.S. oil well was drilled in Pennsylvania in 1859, petroleum supplies were limited to crude oil that oozed to the surface. In 1855, an advertisement for Kier's Rock Oil advised consumers to "hurry, before this wonderful product is depleted from Nature's laboratory."
- In 1874, the state geologist of Pennsylvania, the nation's leading oil-producing state, estimated that only enough U.S. oil remained to keep the nation's kerosene lamps burning for four years.

Seven such oil shortage scares occurred before 1950. As a writer in the *Oil Trade Journal* noted in 1918:

> At regularly recurring intervals in the quarter of a century that I have been following the ins and outs of the oil business[,] there has always arisen the bugaboo of an approaching oil famine, with plenty of individuals ready to prove that the commercial supply of crude oil would become exhausted within a given time—usually only a few years distant.

The 1973 Arab oil embargo gave rise to renewed claims that the world's oil supply would be exhausted shortly. "The Oil Crisis: This Time the Wolf Is Here," warned an article in the influential journal *Foreign Affairs*. Geologists had cried wolf many times, acknowledged the authors of a respected and widely used textbook on economic geology in 1981; "finally, however, the wolves are with us." The authors predicted that the United

States was entering an incipient 125-year-long "energy gap," projected to be at its worst shortly after the year 2000.

The predictions of the 1970s were followed in a few years by a glut of cheap oil:

- The long-term inflation-adjusted price of oil from 1880 through 1970 averaged $10 to $20 a barrel.
- The price of oil soared to over $50 a barrel in inflation-adjusted 1996 U.S. dollars following the 1979 political revolution in Iran.
- But by 1986, inflation-adjusted oil prices had collapsed to one-third their 1980 peak.

When projected crises failed to occur, doomsayers moved their predictions forward by a few years and published again in more visible and prestigious journals:

- In 1989, one expert forecast that world oil production would peak that very year and oil prices would reach $50 a barrel by 1994.
- In 1995, a respected geologist predicted in *World Oil* that petroleum production would peak in 1996, and after 1999 major increases in crude oil prices would have dire consequences. He warned that "[m]any of the world's developed societies may look more like today's Russia than the U.S."
- A 1998 *Scientific American* article entitled "The End of Cheap Oil" predicted that world oil production would peak in 2002 and warned that "what our society does face, and soon, is the end of the abundant and cheap oil on which all industrial nations depend."

Similar admonitions were published in the two most influential scientific journals in the world, *Nature* and *Science*. A 1998 article in *Science* was titled "The Next Oil Crisis Looms Large—and Perhaps Close." A 1999 *Nature* article was subtitled "[A] permanent decline in global oil production rate is virtually certain to begin within 20 years."

> *Rather than ending, the Oil Age has barely begun.*

However, rather than falling, world oil production continued to increase throughout the 1990s. Prices have not skyrock-

eted, suggesting that oil is not becoming more scarce:
- Oil prices were generally stable at $20 to $30 a barrel throughout the 1990s.
- In 2001, oil prices fell to a 30-year low after adjusting for inflation.
- Furthermore, the inflation-adjusted retail price of gasoline, one of the most important derivatives of oil, fell to historic lows in the past few years.

Reserves Versus Resources

Nonexperts, including some in the media, persistently predict oil shortage because they misunderstand petroleum terminology. Oil geologists speak of both reserves and resources.
- *Reserves* are the portion of *identified* resources that can be economically extracted and exploited using current technology.
- *Resources* include all fuels, both identified and unknown, and constitute the world's endowment of fossil fuels.

Oil reserves are analogous to food stocks in a pantry. If a household divides its pantry stores by the daily food consumption rate, the same conclusion is always reached: the family will starve to death in a few weeks. Famine never occurs because the family periodically restocks the pantry.

> *Prices have not skyrocketed, suggesting that oil is not becoming more scarce.*

Similarly, if oil reserves are divided by current production rates, exhaustion appears imminent. However, petroleum reserves are continually increased by ongoing exploration and development of resources. For 80 years, oil reserves in the United States have been equal to a 10- to 14-year supply at current rates of development. If they had not been continually replenished, we would have run out of oil by 1930.

How Much Oil Is Left?

Scaremongers are fond of reminding us that the total amount of oil in the Earth is finite and cannot be replaced during the span of human life. This is true; yet estimates of the world's total oil endowment have grown faster than humanity can pump petroleum out of the ground.

Estimates of the total amount of oil resources in the world grew throughout the 20th century.

- In May 1920, the U.S. Geological Survey announced that the world's total endowment of oil amounted to 60 billion barrels.
- In 1950, geologists estimated the world's total oil endowment at around 600 billion barrels.
- From 1970 through 1990, their estimates increased to between 1,500 and 2,000 billion barrels.
- In 1994, the U.S. Geological Survey raised the estimate to 2,400 billion barrels, and their most recent estimate (2000) was of a 3,000-billion-barrel endowment.

By the year 2000, a total of 900 billion barrels of oil had been produced. Total world oil production in 2000 was 25 billion barrels. If world oil consumption continues to increase at an average rate of 1.4 percent a year, and no further resources are discovered, the world's oil supply will not be exhausted until the year 2056.

Unconventional oil resources are very large.

The estimates above do not include unconventional oil resources. *Conventional* oil refers to oil that is pumped out of the ground with minimal processing; *unconventional* oil resources consist largely of tar sands and oil shales that require processing to extract liquid petroleum. Unconventional oil resources are very large. In the future, new technologies that allow extraction of these unconventional resources likely will increase the world's reserves.

- Oil production from tar sands in Canada and South America would add about 600 billion barrels to the world's supply.
- Rocks found in the three western states of Colorado, Utah and Wyoming alone contain 1,500 billion barrels of oil.
- Worldwide, the oil-shale resource base could easily be as large as 14,000 billion barrels—more than 500 years of oil supply at year 2000 production rates.

Unconventional oil resources are more expensive to extract and produce, but we can expect production costs to drop with time as improved technologies increase efficiency.

The Role of Technology

With every passing year it becomes possible to exploit oil resources that could not have been recovered with old technologies. The first American oil well drilled in 1859 by Colonel Edwin Drake in Titusville, Pa.—which was actually drilled by a local blacksmith known as Uncle Billy Smith—reached a total depth of 69 feet (21 meters).

- Today's drilling technology allows the completion of wells up to 30,000 feet (9,144 meters) deep.
- The vast petroleum resources of the world's submerged continental margins are accessible from offshore platforms that allow drilling in water depths to 9,000 feet (2,743 meters).
- The amount of oil recoverable from a single well has greatly increased because new technologies allow the boring of multiple horizontal shafts from a single vertical shaft.
- Four-dimensional seismic imaging enables engineers and geologists to see a subsurface petroleum reservoir drain over months to years, allowing them to increase the efficiency of its recovery.

New techniques and new technology have increased the efficiency of oil exploration. The success rate for exploratory petroleum wells has increased 50 percent over the past decade, according to energy economist Michael C. Lynch.

Hubbert's Prediction of Declining Production

Despite these facts, some environmentalists claim that declining oil production is inevitable, based on the so-called Hubbert model of energy production. They ignore the inaccuracy of Hubbert's projections.

In March 1956, M. King Hubbert, a research scientist for Shell Oil, predicted that oil production from the 48 contiguous United States would peak between 1965 and 1970. Hubbert's prediction was initially called "utterly ridiculous." But when U.S. oil production peaked in 1970, he became an instant celebrity and living legend.

Hubbert based his estimate on a mathematical model that assumes the production of a resource follows a bell-shaped curve—one that rises rapidly to a peak and declines just as quickly. In the case of petroleum, the model requires an accurate estimate of the size of the total oil endowment. His best estimate of the size of petroleum resources in the lower 48 states was 150 billion barrels. His high estimate, which he considered an exaggeration, was 200 billion barrels.

> *No one can predict the future, but the world contains enough petroleum resources to last at least until the year 2100.*

Based on these numbers, Hubbert produced two curves showing a "best" estimate of U.S. oil production and a "high" estimate. The claimed accuracy of Hubbert's predictions are largely based on the upper curve—his absolute upper limit.

- Hubbert set the absolute upper limit for peak U.S. oil production at roughly 3 billion barrels a year, and his best or lower estimate of peak future U.S. crude oil production was closer to 2.5 billion barrels.
- As early as 1970, actual U.S. crude oil production exceeded Hubbert's upper limit by 13 percent.
- By the year 2000, actual U.S. oil production from the lower 48 states was 2.5 times higher than Hubbert's 1956 "best" prediction.

Production in the 48 contiguous states peaked, but at much higher levels than Hubbert predicted. From about 1975 through 1995, Hubbert's upper curve was a fairly good match to actual U.S. production data. But in recent years, U.S. crude oil production has been consistently higher than Hubbert considered possible.

Hubbert's 1980 prediction of U.S. oil production, his last, was substantially less accurate than his 1956 "high" estimate. In the year 2000, actual U.S. oil production from the lower 48 states was 1.7 times higher than his 1980 revised prediction.

In light of this, it is strange that Hubbert's predictions have been characterized as remarkably successful. While production in the United States is declining, as Hubbert predicted, it is doing so at a much slower rate. Furthermore, lower production does not necessarily indicate the looming exhaustion of U.S. oil resources. It shows instead that at current prices and with current technology, less of the remaining petroleum is economically recoverable.

In 1998, Peter McCabe of the U.S. Geological Survey showed that energy resources do not necessarily follow Hubbert-type curves, and even if they do a decline in production may not be due to exhaustion of the resource.

For example, Hubbert also predicted future U.S. natural gas production. This prediction turned out to be grossly wrong. As of 2000, U.S. natural gas production was 2.4 times higher than Hubbert had predicted in 1956.

The Production Curve for Coal

Production of anthracite coal in Pennsylvania through the 19th and 20th centuries followed a Hubbert-type curve more closely than any other known energy resource. Production started around 1830, peaked around 1920, and by 1995 had fallen to about 5 percent of its peak value. However, the supply of Pennsylvania anthracite coal is far from exhausted. If production were to resume at the all-time high rate of 100 million short tons per year, the resource base would support 190 years of production. Production declined not because the resource was depleted but because people stopped heating their homes with coal and switched to cleaner-burning oil and gas.

The primary problem with a Hubbert-type analysis is that it requires an accurate estimate of the total resource endowment. Yet estimates of the total endowment have grown systematically larger for at least 50 years as technology has made it possible to exploit petroleum resources previously not considered economical. Hubbert-type analyses of oil production have systematically underestimated future oil production. This will continue to be the case until geologists can produce an accurate and stable estimate of the size of the total oil endowment.

In the long run, an economy that utilizes petroleum as a primary energy source is not sustainable, because the amount of oil in the Earth's crust is finite. However, *sustainability* is a misleading concept, a chimera. No technology since the birth of civilization has been sustainable. All have been replaced as people devised better and more efficient technologies. The history of energy use is largely one of substitution. In the 19th century, the world's primary energy source was wood. Around

1890, wood was replaced by coal. Coal remained the world's largest source of energy until the 1960s when it was replaced by oil. We have only just entered the petroleum age.

How long will it last? No one can predict the future, but the world contains enough petroleum resources to last at least until the year 2100. This is so far in the future that it would be ludicrous for us to try to anticipate what energy sources our descendants will utilize. Over the next several decades the world likely will continue to see short-term spikes in the price of oil, but these will be caused by political instability and market interference—not by an irreversible decline in supply.

3

Increasing Government Fuel Efficiency Standards Will Help America Avoid an Energy Crisis

Ralph Nader

Ralph Nader is the founder of many consumer advocacy groups and was the Independent Party presidential candidate for the 2004 presidential elections.

The U.S. government needs to raise Corporate Average Fuel Economy (CAFE) standards. The standards were implemented in 1978 at a shamefully low level of 18 miles per gallon. Today, the average fleet efficiency level is just 27.5 mpg, the lowest level since 1980. The nation has the resources and technical ingenuity to significantly raise these standards. Unfortunately, the automobile industry has consistently resisted the increases and the government has been lax. The time has come to update CAFE standards.

T.S. Eliot once wrote, "April is the cruelest month. . . ." He wasn't referring to the unfilled promise of The New York Auto Show—which is featuring "advances" in automotive engineering this week [April 11, 2004] at the Javits Convention Center in New York City. But anyone who has visited this event knows—the distance between the potential of fuel efficiency and the reality of fuel efficiency is as vast as it is cruel.

Ralph Nader, "The CAFE Standards," *In the Public Interest*, www.nader.org, April 11, 2004. Copyright © 2004 by The Nader Page. Reproduced by permission.

⌈The "Energy Policy Conservation Act," (EPCA) was enacted into law in 1975 and established Corporate Average Fuel Economy (CAFE) standards for passenger cars and light trucks. The goal of the EPCA was to double fuel economy by model year 1985.⌋

The CAFE standards started at a shamefully low level in 1978 when auto companies selling cars in the United States were first required to meet a meager 18 mile per gallon (mpg) auto fleet standard. In 1981 Joan Claybrook, now the President of Public Citizen, was the Administrator of the National Highway Traffic Safety Administration (NHTSA). As the administration of President Jimmy Carter was winding down, Claybrook advanced a NHTSA notice that called for fuel efficiency standards to reach 48 mpg by 1995. Interestingly the notice pointed out that the auto industry itself said it could reach in excess of 30 mpg fuel economy by 1985 with GM saying it could do 33 mpg. The Reagan Administration didn't waste any time and withdrew the NHTSA notice just three months after it was issued. After the original Congressional mandate of 27.5 mpg took effect in 1985, the Reagan Administration rolled the standard back to 26 mpg in 1986. Finally in 1989 the first Bush Administration moved the standard back to the 1985 level of 27.5 mpg. There was no improvement in the CAFE standards under the Clinton Administration.

Fuel Efficiency Is Ignored by Washington

The Bush/Cheney Energy plan of 2001 put off raising CAFE standards. In 2002, Senators John Kerry (D-MA), and John McCain (R-AZ) offered an amendment to the "National Fuel Savings and Security Act of 2002." The amendment called for fuel economy standards for cars and light trucks, beginning with model year 2005, to reach a combined average fuel economy standard of at least 36 miles per gallon by 2015. This amendment lost.

The pork barrel energy bill of 2003 didn't improve the fuel efficiency standards and was too offensive to consumer and environmental and taxpayer groups to even make it out of Congress. NHTSA has advocated raising fuel economy standards for sport utility vehicles (SUVs), minivans, and pickup trucks a whopping 1.5 mpg by 2007. But, the average fleet efficiency levels in new vehicles have slipped to the lowest level since 1980.

So, here we are in 2004, almost twenty years later, and the standard is at the same pitifully low 27.5 mpg level for passenger cars and 20.7 mpg for light trucks and vans. Well it is time for a little introspection.

Is the price of gasoline so low consumers don't mind driving gas guzzlers? The Department of Energy says the retail price of gasoline in the United States is $1.78. At this price even the least frugal consumers have a real incentive to want fuel efficient automobiles.

> *Fuel efficiency standards are stuck in the mud because the auto industry is obstinate and because our elected officials are docile.*

Does our country lack the engineering talent to produce fuel efficient vehicles? There are, after all, only 185 engineering schools with doctoral programs and only about 330 colleges and universities that offer bachelor's degree programs in engineering in the United States. I suspect we have abundant engineering talent.

Could it be our Gross Domestic Product of $10.45 trillion is too small to provide the base needed to create a market for fuel efficient cars?

Not likely—in 2003 GM's total revenue was $186.8 billion and Ford's revenue was $164.2 billion.

Could it be that auto fuel efficiency is too small an item in our nation's energy mix? Not according to the American Council for an Energy Efficient Economy—they note transportation accounts for 28 percent of U.S. energy consumption and "over three-quarters of transportation energy use is by highway vehicles—60 percent by cars and light trucks (including minivans and sport utility vehicles)."

Fuel efficiency standards are stuck in the mud because the auto industry is obstinate and because our elected officials are docile.

It's Time for Action in Washington

For years, the U.S. auto industry, and the government, have produced "promising prototype" cars which have gone nowhere. Toyota and Honda are starting to make inroads with their gas/electric Hybrid cars. It is time to update the CAFE standards, improve air pollution requirements and spark competition in the marketplace to stimulate the production of cars with greatly reduced environmental impacts.

Congress should require the CAFE standard be raised to at least 45 mpg for cars and 35 mpg for light trucks, to be phased in over five years.

The auto industry has had almost 20 years to gear up for this schedule, given their bragging about their Research & Development programs.

Consumers will save money at the pump, the air we breathe will be cleaner, and the amount of oil we import will decrease. For more information on fuel efficiency vs. safety visit: http://www.Citizen.org. We can start brightening our energy future by strengthening our fuel efficiency standards—even Detroit has had enough lead time to catch up with Tokyo.

4

Increasing Government Fuel Efficiency Standards Will Not Lead to Fuel Conservation

Andrew Kleit

Andrew Kleit is a professor of energy and environmental economics at Pennsylvania State University.

Proponents of increasing Corporate Average Fuel Economy (CAFE) standards claim that these standards are the best and easiest way to reduce gasoline consumption. However, the costs of stricter CAFE standards far outweigh the benefits. While some fuel will be saved by improved efficiency, some of these savings will be lost through increased driving. As the actual cost of driving goes down because of improved efficiency, demand for driving rises, resulting in more fuel consumption. The most effective way to reduce gasoline consumption is through taxation.

[In 2002], the U.S. Senate considered a proposal by Sen. John Kerry (D-Mass.) to raise the Corporate Average Fuel Economy (CAFE) standards for cars and light trucks by 50 percent. Kerry and other proponents of stricter standards had the support of a July 2001 report by the National Research Council (NRC) that called for significantly higher standards, as well as the backing of many major newspapers. The [September 11, 2001, terrorist attacks] and the subsequent resurgence of violence and political uncertainty in the Mideast added to the momentum in favor of new fuel efficiency standards. But a coalition of Republicans and auto-state Democrats defeated the Kerry measure by a decisive and surprising 62-38 vote.

To the casual observer, the decision may have seemed a defeat of the public interest by special interests. In fact, it was a victory for economic common sense. As many economists and other policy experts have argued, the CAFE standards save very little gasoline, increase car buyers' costs and lower their benefits, increase pollution and auto fatalities, and shift revenue away from U.S. automakers to foreign firms. Instead of raising the fuel efficiency standards, policymakers would better address any externalities associated with gasoline by raising the gas tax.

A Brief History of CAFE

The CAFE program, enacted in 1975, required all manufacturers selling more than 10,000 autos per year in the United States to have sales-weighted fuel economy of 19.0 miles per gallon in 1978. That meant that all of the new cars that an automaker sold had to average 19 mpg, though individual models could have gas mileages below that level. Under the law, the mileage standard increased to 27.5 mpg in 1985, and it currently remains at that level.

The CAFE law divides an automaker's cars into foreign and domestic fleets. It also offered a different standard for light trucks (pickup trucks, sport-utility vehicles, and minivans)—a concession that seemed insignificant in 1975 because those vehicles comprised only a small percentage of the total number of vehicles on the road. However, that concession has become increasingly significant in recent years as light truck sales—buoyed by the wildly popular sport-utility vehicle—now comprise nearly half of all U.S. auto sales. The National Highway Transportation Safety Administration, using authority granted it through CAFE, currently requires a 20.7-mpg fleet-efficiency standard for light trucks, but the agency is considering raising that standard.

Compliance If a manufacturer does riot comply with the CAFE standards, it is subject to a civil fine of $55 per car/mpg. For example, if a manufacturer produces one million cars with a sales-weighted mpg of 26.5 mpg, that firm could be subject to a fine of $55 per car/mpg × 1 million cars × 1 mpg, or $55 million.

Foreign automakers view the fine as a tax. Thus, BMW and Mercedes-Benz, for example, have routinely paid CAFE fines. In contrast, American firms view the standards as binding because their lawyers have advised them that, if they violate CAFE, they would be liable for civil damages in stockholder suits. The fear of civil suit is so strong that even Chrysler, which is owned by the German firm Daimler-Benz, will not violate the limits. Because the "shadow tax" of the CAFE constraint (the cost of complying with the standards rather than paying the fine) can be much more than $55 per car/mpg, the effects of CAFE standards are much larger on U.S. automakers than foreign firms.

Gasoline Externalities

In a free market, consumers equate the price of a commodity (the "internal" cost) with the marginal value of its consumption. In the absence of any external costs like air pollution or traffic congestion, the marginal value of a gallon of gas to consumers equals its price. No public benefit would arise from reducing the consumption of gasoline, under that scenario. However, if external costs do exist, economic theory recommends that the appropriate policy response is to increase the price to consumers to equal the marginal cost of production plus the cost of the externality. That way, the consumer must consider the full cost of the commodity when he purchases and uses it.

> *Foreign automakers stand to draw a lot of profits away from U.S. firms if stricter CAFE standards are adopted.*

That leads to an important question: Does gasoline consumption create external effects that consumers do not currently pay for? As part of its research on CAFE, the NRC estimated that the external costs associated with the consumption of a gallon of gasoline are approximately 26¢ per gallon. The NRC reached that figure by estimating that the combustion of the gas produces 12¢ worth of adverse global climate effects, 12¢ worth of detrimental oil-import effects, and 2¢ worth of undesirable changes from pollution emissions from refineries.

The cost estimates are subject to several criticisms. With respect to climate change, there is a wide range of uncertainty about measuring the relevant externality. Previous estimates have placed it between 1¢ and 4¢ a gallon, implying the NRC may have overestimated the cost by a factor of at least three. The oil-import effects estimate can be criticized for ignoring the theory of comparative advantage, which holds that those who can produce a certain good at the lowest cost should be the ones to produce it. Thus, it makes far more sense for oil to be produced in Saudi Arabia at $2 a barrel rather than Alaska at $20 a barrel. Granted, some argue that reducing U.S. consumption of imported oil would make the United States economically more secure, but that assertion ignores the fact that the market for oil is worldwide and we cannot isolate ourselves from any price shock.

Despite those criticisms, let us assume that the NRC estimates are correct. The policy implication is that government should affix a 26¢ externality tax on a gallon of gasoline. Of course, gasoline already is taxed significantly, but under federal law most of the funds from the existing tax are used to build and maintain roadways, and therefore should be viewed as user fees rather than attempts to combat externalities. Those taxes, ironically, work to encourage more driving and gasoline usage. An externality tax should be assessed in addition to the roadway tax, to cover the external costs produced by the gasoline. The revenue generated from the tax should then be spent on projects other than road construction.

CAFE supporters claim that such a tax is politically unfeasible. I disagree with that opinion; the federal government, every single state in the union, and all developed foreign countries of which I am aware have gasoline taxes. The average tax (federal and state combined) on gasoline in the United States is currently 41¢ per gallon. Democratically elected European governments have much higher taxes. Hence, it does not seem that an additional tax on gasoline is politically unfeasible.

Problems with CAFE

Ignoring concerns over feasibility, CAFE proponents claim that increasing the fuel efficiency standards has the added advantage of creating net benefits apart from any reduction in the external cost of gasoline use. The NRC report goes so far as to assert that higher standards would actually pay for themselves, with the increased costs more than offset by reduced fuel con-

38

sumption—yet another "free lunch" from Washington, D.C.

Contrary to those claims, it appears that stricter standards would save very little gasoline. There are three basic reasons for that:

- CAFE has only a limited effect on the production of "gas-guzzlers."
- CAFE leads to increased driving.
- CAFE keeps older cars with lower gas mileage on the road.

Gas-guzzlers The CAFE standards affect the mix of vehicles produced by a manufacturer, but not the overall production of any particular type of car. That is important to remember because, as explained earlier, domestic firms will feel constrained by the new standards but foreign firms will not. The constrained U.S. firms will be forced to increase their fuel efficiency, leaving an undersupply in the large-car market. In turn, foreign firms will move into that market and begin producing vehicles with lower fuel efficiency. Though the cars will have a slightly higher price because of CAFE fines, they likely will still appeal to consumers, so the overall mix of cars being sold will not change nearly as much as what CAFE proponents expect.

> *Increased CAFE standards also result in more auto fatalities.*

Foreign automakers stand to draw a lot of profits away from U.S. firms if stricter CAFE standards are adopted. Honda and Toyota, for example, have fleet averages now that likely would satisfy any new standards that Congress might pass, hence the automakers would have no disincentive to try for a larger share of the U.S. large-car market. (In fact, they may feel they need to move into that market because U.S. automakers will be moving into the small-car market.) Even if the foreign automakers' fleet averages would not satisfy the new standards, the automakers likely would pay the relatively small mileage fines in order to have a larger share of the market.

More driving CAFE standards may reduce the consumption of fuel per mile, but they also increase the overall amount of driving. Because the standards lower the per-mile cost of operating a car, drivers have less financial incentive to drive less. Vehicle use is just like any other market in which demand is responsive to price: A decrease in cost results in an increase in aggregate use. The latest estimates are that for every 10 percent increase in fuel efficiency, people increase their driving by two percent. Those trends indicate, again, that the fuel savings from tighter CAFE standards will be less than what proponents believe.

> **❝** *If the fuel efficiency standards were to be increased 3 mpg . . . U.S. consumer surplus would decline $1.841 billion.* **❞**

Old cars By raising the cost of new cars, CAFE standards provide a disincentive for old-car owners to trade in their lower-gas-mileage vehicles for new, more-efficient ones. That, in turn, increases gasoline consumption by older cars because they will be staying on the road instead of being taken to the scrap yards. So, yet again, stricter CAFE standards will have less of a gas-saving effect than what proponents claim.

Other problems CAFE standards not only save very little gasoline, they increase air pollutants such as volatile organic compounds (VOC), oxides of nitrogen (NO_x), and carbon monoxide (CO). The increases occur because the standards do not alter a car's grams/mile of emissions and thus do nothing to alter pollution levels directly. Because the pollution from a car is a direct function of the number of miles it is driven, and people in more fuel-efficient vehicles drive more, the net result from an increase in CAFE standards is an increase in automobile pollutants.

Increased CAFE standards also result in more auto fatalities. As the NRC panel conceded in its report, compliance with stricter standards means that automakers lighten their cars. Lighter, smaller cars, in turn, mean more fatalities from automobile accidents.

Finally, CAFE standards are, in large part, unworkable because demand can shift much more quickly than a manufacturer's ability to alter the fuel use of its vehicles. For example, it would take a firm three to five years to re-engineer its cars so that, at current demand levels, the fleet would satisfy a new standard. But consumers can change their buying habits in an extremely short period of time and can buy a mix of cars very different than what automakers expected. Automakers, through no fault of their own, could face short-run CAFE problems that they could address only through "mix-shifting"—selling fewer large cars and more small cars by raising prices on the former and lowering them on the latter. Because mix-shifting annoys consumers and reduces industry employment, the government has little choice but to grant the automakers relief, or else the politicians will permit serious unemployment and economic harm.

These considerations further indicate that the benefits of new CAFE standards will be less, and the negative effects more, than what proponents believe.

Effects on Automakers

On behalf of General Motors, I created a model of the impact of stricter CAFE standards on domestic and foreign automakers. I assumed that the relevant period is the "long-run," so as to allow for the development of new technologies that would assist firms in meeting the stricter standards. As part of the model, I considered two different proposals for new CAFE standards: the 3-mpg increase proposed by Vice President Dick Cheney's energy task force and the 50-percent increase proposed by Sen. Kerry. For my cost-benefit analysis, I adopted the NRC assumption that the level of externality associated with a gallon of gasoline is 26¢, despite my reservations about that figure. . . .

Cheney proposal I found that increasing the CAFE standards by 3 mpg would reduce annual profits at General Motors by $433 million, at Ford by $455 million, and at Chrysler by $236 million. Total losses to U.S. automakers would amount to $1.124 billion. In contrast, foreign manufacturers would see an increase in profits of $260 million.

With respect to consumers, losses are measured in terms of the economic concept of "consumer surplus." For example, assume a consumer values a car for $20,000, and is able to purchase it for $18,000. That consumer would gain $2,000 in consumer surplus. If CAFE standards make that car unavailable and the consumer chooses not to purchase a car, the new standards would have caused a loss of $2,000 in consumer surplus for that consumer. If the fuel efficiency standards were to be increased 3 mpg, I estimate that U.S. consumer surplus would decline $1.841 billion.

Emissions of all three "criteria" pollutants would increase relative to emissions if the CAFE standards remained unchanged. Increasing the standards by 3 MPG would increase VOC emissions by 1.64 percent, NO_x emissions by 1.80 percent, and CO emissions by 1.86 percent. The new standards would result in a decrease in consumption of 5.091 billion gallons, or about 7.15 percent of fleet consumption. The marginal cost of a gallon of gasoline saved would be $1.06.

Kerry proposal Increasing the CAFE standards by 50 percent would cause far more harm to the economy. I estimate that passage of the Kerry proposal would have reduced annual profits at General Motors by $3.824 billion, at Ford by $3.423 billion, and at Chrysler by $1.959 billion. Total losses to U.S. automakers would amount to $9.206 billion. In contrast, foreign manufacturers would see an increase in profits of $4.434 billion. Consumer surplus would decline $17.603 billion.

Emissions of all three "criteria" pollutants would increase above what would occur if the CAFE standards remained unchanged. Increasing fuel efficiency as proposed would increase VOC emissions by 1.87 percent, NO_x emissions by 3.41 percent, and CO emissions by 4.57 percent. The new standards would result in a decrease in consumption of 14.690 billion gallons, or about 20.6 percent of fleet consumption. The marginal cost of a gallon of gasoline saved would be $3.93.

> *If policymakers wish to reduce energy consumption, they should tax gasoline consumption.*

Given the estimates generated by my model, what are the costs and benefits of the two CAFE proposals? Let us assume, as the NRC indicates, that the external cost of the consumption of a gallon of gasoline is 26¢ per gallon—which would thus be the benefit from a gallon of gasoline not consumed. My model indicates that the average cost of a 3-mpg increase in fuel standards is 2.2 (58¢ ÷ 26¢) times the benefits. The average cost of a 50-percent increase in the standards is about 6.5 ($1.68 ÷ 26¢) times the benefits. The marginal cost of the Cheney proposal would be 4.1 ($1.06 ÷ 26¢) times the benefits. And the marginal cost of the Kerry proposal is 15.1 times ($3.93 ÷ 26¢) times the benefits.

Proponents of stricter CAFE standards, including the authors of the recent NRC report, claim that increasing the CAFE standards is the policy equivalent of a free lunch. But fuel efficiency standards are an extremely poor policy tool. If enforced, they would reduce consumer welfare and motorist safety, harm the environment, and increase the profits of foreign firms. Worst of all, they do not save gasoline very effectively.

If policymakers wish to reduce energy consumption, they should tax gasoline consumption. It is that simple. Unfortunately, altering the CAFE standards is a politically attractive policy to invoke to reduce gasoline consumption's external costs. Because of that attractiveness, there is little debate on the real issues involved in energy consumption.

5

Drilling in the Arctic National Wildlife Refuge Would Reduce U.S. Dependence on Foreign Oil

Larry E. Craig

Larry E. Craig is a U.S. senator from Idaho.

Cheap and reliable energy is the lifeblood of any flourishing and stable economy. As gas prices continue to rise and political instability in the Middle East worsens, the United States must increase its domestic oil production. The Arctic National Wildlife Refuge (ANWR) in Alaska is estimated to have as much as 16 billion barrels of oil under its coastal plain. Drilling in ANWR will add to national economic output, create jobs, and improve national energy security. Moreover, it will not disrupt the natural habitat of Alaska.

In [an] appearance on "Meet the Press," Sen. John Kerry (D.-Mass.) indicated he was "ready to negotiate" on the CAFE (Corporate Average Fuel Economy) standards that he has proposed in legislation that would raise the average fuel economy standards to 36 miles per gallon (mpg) on the automotive industry. With rising gasoline prices hitting consumers at the pump and continued instability in the Middle East, I have tried to make energy production a point of debate this year in the U.S. Senate.

The President, as most Americans know, understood when he took office that our nation's powerful economy is dependent on cheap and reliable energy and that our growing dependence on foreign sources of energy threatened the stability of our economy—indeed, threatened our national security. Upon taking office he quickly assigned the Vice President [Dick Cheney] to review the status of both world energy markets and our domestic energy needs. The Vice President swiftly and comprehensively completed the task and the President, in May 2001, published his National Energy Policy.

> *Pumping such vast oil resources to the surface would reduce America's dependence on foreign oil.*

The document contained 105 suggested actions aimed at overhauling our nation's energy policy. More than half of the domestic recommendations in that document are focused on conservation, environmental protection, renewable and alternative energy production, and measures to assist consumers hurt by high-energy prices. The energy bill currently stalled in Congress adopted those recommendations.

Democratic Opposition

Apparently, that was not enough for Sen. Kerry and many other Senate Democrats that continue to oppose energy legislation by refusing to allow an up or down vote on the pending Conference Report for HR 6, "The Energy Policy Act of 2003."[1] Ironically, that bill does have a majority in the Senate supporting the bill.

President [George W.] Bush and Sen. Kerry have starkly different views of how best to improve the quantity and reliability of America's energy supplies. For proof, let's take a look at the key elements of their energy proposals. President Bush supports exploration of the Arctic National Wildlife Refuge (ANWR) to

---

1. The bill did not pass, and Kerry's amendment lost.

make use of untapped oil resources in the region. Sen. Kerry favors increasing Corporate Average Fuel Economy, or CAFE, mandates. Deeper examination of those policies shows us that President Bush has a more reliable plan for overcoming the energy challenges America now faces.

Raising CAFE standards would not increase America's energy supply by a single barrel. The possible benefits of higher CAFE standards depend on the reduced use of gasoline in cars. The government measures the fuel economy of every automobile that enters the U.S. market (the number is marked on the sticker you find on new cars) and mandates that the average fuel economy across an automotive company's entire fleet of cars meet a certain target—currently 24 mpg. Sen. Kerry's plan is to raise that average to 36 mpg, in hopes it would lead to less oil consumption in the United States.

Untapped Oil

On the other hand, the U.S. Department of the Interior estimates that at least 9 billion and as many as 16-billion barrels of oil lie untapped under the coastal plain of ANWR. Pumping such vast oil resources to the surface would reduce America's dependence on foreign oil—a situation that currently results in our sending more than $55 billion a year out of America and into oil-producing countries.

Raising CAFE standards or obtaining oil from ANWR would also have a vastly different impact on job creation and economic growth in America.

In a time when our economy is recovering and beginning to add jobs, Sen. Kerry's proposed 50% increase in CAFE standards would cost jobs and reduce economic output. The government's Energy Information Administration estimates that Kerry's increase would lead to 450,000 job losses—most concentrated in the automotive industry. Those massive job losses explain why the United Auto Workers are firmly opposed to raising CAFE standards as drastically as Sen. Kerry proposes.

In addition to job losses, higher CAFE standards would result in $170 billion in lost economic output. Losses to U.S. automakers alone are estimated at about $9 billion.

In contrast, tapping into the oil reserves in ANWR would produce jobs through the construction of temporary facilities to access the coastal plain and to bring up the oil from deep under the surface. American workers would build those facilities and American workers would operate the pumps. All told, developing oil production facilities on the ANWR coastal plain would generate anywhere from 250,000 to more than 700,000 jobs. Unlike Kerry's plan, major labor unions have endorsed the President's plan for ANWR exploration.

> **//** *Despite arguments to the contrary, oil production in ANWR would pose little threat to the habitat and animals of Alaska.* **//**

Those jobs and the oil we bring to market would also have an extraordinarily positive impact on America's economy. From 1980 to 1994, oil production on the North Slope of Alaska added more than $50 billion to our nation's economy and directly benefited every state in the union. Oil production in ANWR would likely produce equal or greater economic gains.

Higher CAFE standards also pose potential threats to highway safety. Because CAFE by definition mandates certain "average fuel economy" levels, the fuel economy of individual cars in any automaker's fleet may fall above or below that level. Americans love sport utility vehicles (SUVs), which generally get lower fuel economy—often under 20 mpg—and U.S. manufacturers have regained their strong position in the American marketplace by producing SUVs. For that reason, SUVs will continue to be a major presence on American roads.

To balance the low fuel efficiency ratings of SUVs, automakers produce cars with high fuel efficiency—over 30 mpg. The easiest way to do that is to make cars lighter and smaller. However, the drivers of these smaller cars are placed at increasing risk of serious injury or death if they are involved in an accident. The National Academy of Sciences [NAS] found a decade ago that "downweighting" and downsizing vehicles led to as many as 2,600 deaths and 26,000 serious injuries in one year alone. And the NAS stated that "any increase in CAFE as currently structured could produce additional road casualties."

A Minimal Environmental Threat from Drilling

Seizing the oil that lies under the coastal plain of the Arctic National Wildlife Refuge would pose no such threat to American drivers. Despite arguments to the contrary, oil production in ANWR would pose little threat to the habitat and animals of Alaska either. Of ANWR's 19-million acres, less than 10%, or 1.5-million acres, would be affected by development. The rest of ANWR would be permanently closed to development of any kind.

Meanwhile, the caribou who make their home in ANWR show no signs of being adversely affected by development. Rather, they seem to be thriving. During operation of the Prudhoe Bay oil production facilities, numbers of a local caribou herd grew from 3,000 to more than 18,000 two decades into production. And most important, the people of Alaska overwhelmingly support development in ANWR, rejecting the spurious claims of extreme environmental activists who have never lived north of Manhattan.

Developing ANWR to make use of America's own untapped oil resources is a far more preferable method of increasing domestic energy production and decreasing our dependence on foreign oil than is raising CAFE standards. Oil production in ANWR will create jobs, add to national economic output, and bolster U.S. energy supplies without threatening the natural habitat of Alaska—or threatening the safety of American drivers and the health of the U.S. automotive industry and its workers.

President Bush is committed to finding the right solutions to America's energy challenges. On ANWR he's hit the mark.

6

Tapping U.S. Oil Reserves Will Not Reduce America's Dependence on Foreign Oil

William R. Freudenburg

William R. Freudenburg is a professor of rural sociology and environmental studies at the University of Wisconsin in Madison.

Many politicians claim that by increasing U.S. oil production, the nation can restore its energy independence. Unfortunately, these claims are not realistic. The U.S. demand for oil is far too great and continues to increase. Presently, the United States produces less than 10 percent of the global oil supply yet consumes over 25 percent of it. The nation now has just 3 percent of the world's proven oil reserves. Drilling in the United States will never make America energy independent.

It's time for a reality check on energy policy.

Politicians are fond of claiming that increased domestic oil production can restore energy "independence," but anyone who actually believes those claims is living in a world of self-delusion. U.S. energy independence hasn't been physically possible since the days when Elvis was still singing, and if we're talking about oil, it won't ever be possible again.

There are two reasons. One is that the United States simply

uses too much oil, too wastefully. The other is that we've already burned up almost all the petroleum we have. The calls for "energy independence" aren't based on realism; they're based on nostalgia.

U.S. Petroleum History

To be fair, we've had quite a petroleum history. Back in 1859, the United States was the country where the idea of drilling for oil originated, and for nearly a century thereafter, we were a virtual one-nation OPEC [Organization of Petroleum Exporting Countries]. Save for a few years around the turn of the last century, the United States produced over half of all the oil in the world more or less continuously until 1953.

> **"** *It is no longer possible for the United States to drill its way to energy independence.* **"**

But ever since then, our proportion of world oil production has been dropping, with only minor fluctuations, no matter how much our politicians have tried to stop the slide. Ironically, around 1973, when President Nixon's "Project Independence" first brought the issue of energy policy (and the idea of energy "independence") to the minds of most Americans, the country moved decisively in just the opposite direction from independence. Even during the massive push to increase U.S. oil production in the years of Ronald Reagan and James Watt, the only real effect was a tiny increase in the U.S. proportion of world oil production—from 14.5 percent to 16.8 percent—between 1980 and 1985.

By the time Reagan left office, physical reality had reappeared, and the U.S. share of world oil production was even lower than when he started. In recent years, we have produced less than a tenth of the world's oil.

Why have politicians been arguing about oil exploration on the northern edge of Alaska, even as we keep moving farther off the southern edge of the continent, into the ever-deeper waters of the Gulf of Mexico? It's simple: We've already drained almost everything in between.

Politically savvy spin doctors may be able to get many Americans to overlook the facts, at least in the short run, but they aren't going to change reality, and they aren't going to turn back the clock. According to the American Petroleum Institute, the United States is now down to just 3 percent of the world's proven reserves of oil. Wishful thinking isn't going to change that.

Unless the politicians can figure out how to turn their hot air into oil, we need to face the facts: It is no longer possible for the United States to drill its way to energy independence. This country simply doesn't have that much oil left, and if we use that oil faster, we will just run out sooner.

Only if we recognize the facts can we start to talk about a realistic energy policy. If the United States is ever to become energy-independent again, it won't be because of oil.

7
Renewable Alternatives to Fossil Fuels Are Necessary

Dohn Riley

Dohn Riley is author of Turning the Corner: Energy Solutions for the 21st Century *and a contributor to* Infinite Energy, *a journal dedicated to new forms of energy.*

Fossil fuels—oil, coal, and natural gas—have been the primary sources of world energy throughout the twentieth century. However, relying on these nonrenewable sources is foolish. The supply of these fuels is limited, and they pollute the environment. It is necessary to accelerate the development and adoption of renewable energy sources such as solar and wind power. Because some experts are predicting the world oil supply could be depleted within a few decades, it is imperative to begin transitioning to renewable energy sources now to avoid massive economic disruption caused by a global energy crisis.

Two hundred years ago, the world experienced an energy revolution that launched the Industrial Age. The catalyst to this epochal shift was ordinary black coal, an energy-rich hydrocarbon that supplanted wood as the primary fuel. The energy stored in coal gave inventors and industrialists the power they needed to process steel, propel steamships, and energize machines. A century later, the industrialized world's thirst for energy had increased tremendously. Petroleum and natural gas were exploited as versatile and high quality energy products, and soon joined coal as principal fuels. Fifty years later, scientists tapped uranium to fuel nuclear reactors and provide atomic energy.

Today, cheap energy is the lifeblood of American society. But there is a dangerous dark side to relying on nonrenewable resources like coal, oil, natural gas, or uranium to supply our growing energy demands. The supply of these fuels is physically limited, and their use threatens our health and environment. Fears of global warming aside, burning fossil fuel releases chemicals and particulates that can cause cancer, brain and nerve damage, birth defects, lung injury, and breathing problems. The toxic stew released by combusting hydrocarbons pollutes the air and water, and causes acid rain and smog. Nuclear energy, once touted as "too cheap to meter," has never been economically successful when all costs are factored in, and fear of disasters like the Chernobyl reactor melt-down have virtually shut the industry down in the U.S. and Europe. Inexpensive and seemingly abundant nonrenewable energy fueled the twentieth century economy, but geologists, climatologists, environmentalists, and many others are warning that the honeymoon may soon be over.

Coal: A Leading Pollutant

Coal is the most abundant of the carbon-based fossil fuels, but it is also a leading threat to human health and the environment. Coal currently provides 24% of the world's primary energy requirements and, in 1999, generated 57% of all the electricity used in the U.S. Existing coal reserves may be large, but they won't last forever, and health and environmental costs limit its potential as an acceptable fuel in the future. Burning coal currently accounts for 43% of all annual global carbon emissions, about 2.7 billion tons.

The top ten most air-polluted cities in the world—nine in China, one in India—all use coal as a primary energy source. Atmospheric scientists have tracked large dust clouds of particulates and sulfur from Asia to the United States' west coast. In the U.S., coal reserves surpass those of oil and natural gas by about two hundred years and can be mined domestically, but using coal simply because there is plenty of it would be a serious mistake. Air pollution, acid rain, greenhouse gas emissions, and other health dangers associated with processing coal into electricity take their toll on countless people around the world. Western governments rarely discuss "coal" and the "future" in the same sentence anymore, but burning coal has become a global problem that respects no international boundaries.

> // *The U.S. has 4% of the world's people but slurps down 25% of the world's oil.* //

Cheap and abundant oil is an intoxicating elixir that the world's industrial nations have guzzled down as if there is no tomorrow. Petroleum currently accounts for 40% of the world's energy, but many geologists anticipate an oil supply crisis sometime within the next two decades when global demand will exceed supply. While some argue that huge deposits of oil may lie undetected in far-off locations of the globe, experts point out that there is only so much crude in the world, and industry has found about 90% of it. The world's burgeoning population is dependent on food grown with petroleum-based fertilizers, cultivated by machines running on cheap fuel.

In 1950, the U.S. was producing half the world's oil. Fifty years later, we don't produce half our own oil. Domestic production peaked in 1970. Originally, America was blessed with about 260 billion barrels; only one country, Saudi Arabia, had more. Although the U.S. is now the world's third largest producer, about 65% of our known oil has been burned. It's downhill from here. The U.S. has 4% of the world's people but slurps down 25% of the world's oil. If the Chinese annually consumed oil at the same per capita rate as Americans, there would be none available for anyone else.

Natural Gas: Cleaner but Nonrenewable

Natural gas (methane) is being touted by energy providers as an abundant clean fuel for the twenty-first century. It is forecast to be the fastest growing primary energy source, because it burns cleaner than coal or oil. But this resource is also nonrenewable, and the Department of Energy states that the U.S. has only 3.5% of the world's total natural gas reserves—enough to last about sixty-five years. More than 70% of the world's proven natural gas reserves are located in the politically risky Persian

Gulf and former Soviet Union. After 2020, the bulk of the world's remaining supplies of both oil and natural gas will be centered there.

> *There is little support among Americans and Europeans for fission nuclear energy.*

According to the Energy Information Administration, natural gas provides 27% of the energy used today. Similar to their consumption of oil, Americans consume more than their share of natural gas; in 1997, the U.S. used 28% of the world's total production. Consumption in the U.S. and Canada is expected to grow 50% by 2020, enforced in part by the Clean Air Act Amendments of 1990, which are designed to curb acid rain, toxic emissions, and urban air pollution. Compared to the combustion of oil and coal, natural gas combustion is relatively benign as a contributor to air pollution. American troops have already shed blood in the Middle East protecting our oil interests; relying on natural gas for a primary energy source has similar costs and risks.

Nuclear energy presents similar problems to those associated with nonrenewable fossil fuels. The planet's supply of uranium is limited, and mining the ore is hazardous to human health. Worse, the radioactive waste byproducts are a lethal long-term danger to the environment. In 1999, nuclear energy provided about 17% of the world's electricity, but splitting the atom to boil water is like using a chainsaw to cut butter. The health and environmental costs of using atomic energy have become serious obstacles to the industry. Disposal of radioactive waste has proven to be a much greater problem than originally estimated. Nuclear power does not contribute to air pollution and greenhouse gas emissions, but a good solution to safely storing tons and tons of radioactive waste, a nuclear byproduct that remains dangerous to all life-forms for thousands of years, remains elusive.

Nuclear Energy's Inherent Problems

In the 1950s and 1960s, atomic energy was hailed as an unlimited panacea to the pollution problems generated by fossil fuels, and destined to be so cheap that electric companies wouldn't even put meters on houses. Today, there is little support among Americans and Europeans for fission nuclear energy. Nobody wants a nuclear reactor in their backyard, and frightening publicity regarding reactor meltdowns at Chernobyl and Three Mile Island has only reinforced these fears. Health officials estimate that at least 4,365 people who took part in the Chernobyl cleanup have died in the Ukraine. [Editor's note: These high figures are disputed by some experts.] The risk from nuclear power plants and nuclear-waste disposal sites demands a vigilance and longevity of our social institutions that is unprecedented.

> *Renewable energy will play a major role in the energy industry of the twenty-first century and beyond.*

Coal, natural gas, and uranium are alternative non-renewable energy resources to cheap oil, but each has advantages and limitations, and none is as versatile as petroleum. The replacement of oil will require a mix of energy sources, including clean renewable energy such as solar and wind power. This adjustment will involve substantial reorganization of the world's economic structure and significant lifestyle changes in the industrialized countries.

Economists like to point out that the world contains enormous caches of unconventional oil that can substitute for crude oil as soon as the price becomes competitive. It is true that resources of heavy oil, tar sands, and shale deposits exist in large quantities. But the industry will be hard-pressed for the time and money needed to ramp up production of unconventional oil quickly enough to forestall an economic crisis. Experts who point out the approaching end of Hydrocarbon Man are not pessimists or alarmists; they are simply saying now is the time to plan, lest the end of cheap fossil fuels be an unprecedented disaster in human history.

Renewable Energy: Unlimited and Clean

Renewable energy will play a major role in the energy industry of the twenty-first century and beyond. British Petroleum, Royal

Dutch/Shell, and other companies are investing heavily in renewable sources of energy. Industry experts realize that these alternative energy systems not only help reduce greenhouse gas emissions, but they predict that over the next half century, renewables may grow to supply half the world's energy. Successfully generating electricity by harnessing the perpetual power of the Sun and wind is not only technologically feasible, it is already a reality. Solar power relies on the energy produced by nuclear fusion in the Sun. This energy can be collected and converted in different ways, such as simple water heating for domestic use or by the direct conversion of sunlight to electrical energy using mirrors, boilers, or photovoltaic cells. The technology is improving and the economics are getting more competitive. Photovoltaic panels don't generate electricity at night, but they can be used to produce hydrogen in the daytime, which can then be stored.

Scientists and engineers are continually improving the efficiency of renewable energy systems. Humans have been harnessing the wind for thousands of years, and are now cleanly producing electricity with it. Air flowing through turbines or spinning blades generates power that can be used to pump water or generate electricity. Wind energy is now the world's fastest growing energy source and has become one of the most rapidly expanding industries.

Wind power has some drawbacks; a "wind farm" requires extensive aerial coverage to produce significant amounts of energy, and bird fatalities have been a concern. The wind industry is modifying equipment to address this issue but also points out that countless wild creatures are killed every year as part of the acquisition and distribution of conventional energy sources.

> // Wind energy is now the world's fastest growing energy source. //

Hydroelectric power is another source of renewable energy. Hydroelectric dams, however, are no longer considered environmentally benign sources of power. Fisheries and other wildlife habitat have been severely impacted on many dammed rivers. Most of the world's hydroelectric dams are historically recent, but all reservoirs eventually fill up and require very expensive excavation to become useful again. At this time, most of the available locations for hydroelectric dams in the U.S. are already developed.

> *Producing hydrogen with solar power is the dream of environmentalists and renewable energy proponents.*

Humans have been burning biomass materials since the dawn of time, and it is still the principal fuel used in many parts of the world. Incredibly, just 120 years ago, wood was the chief energy source in the U.S. But today's economy runs on oil, and despite significant government support, converting wood to alcohol, or corn to ethanol has proven neither economical nor energy efficient. Researchers have recently discovered how to produce clean combustible gas from waste products such as sewage and crop residue, but biomass gas will not soon replace petroleum as the fuel of choice.

Hydrogen from Solar Energy

Hydrogen has been touted as the fuel of the future. It is the most abundant element known in the universe and can be burned cleanly as a fuel for vehicles with water as the main combustion byproduct. Hydrogen can also be fed into a fuel cell, a battery-like device that generates heat and electricity. Using hydrogen instead of gasoline or diesel will significantly reduce the health hazards and medical costs associated with the exhaust from conventional internal combustion engines. But the large-scale extraction of hydrogen from terrestrial resources such as water, coal, or natural gas requires a lot of energy, which is currently produced by burning fossil fuels. Commercial hydrogen production is expensive and only shifts the pollution from vehicles back to the power plants. Producing hydrogen with solar power is the dream of environmentalists and renewable energy proponents. If done successfully, hydrogen and electricity will eventually become society's primary energy carriers in the twenty-first century.

Geothermal energy left over from the original accretion radioactive decay seeps out slowly everywhere, everyday. In certain areas, the geothermal gradient (increase in temperature with depth) is high enough to exploit for the generation of electricity. Another form of geothermal energy can be tapped from the planet's surface. Soil maintains a relatively constant temperature throughout the year and can be used with heat pumps to warm a building in winter or cool a dwelling in summer. This form of energy can lessen the need for other power to maintain comfortable temperatures in buildings, but it cannot be used to produce electricity.

Tides, waves, and the heat differential within the world's tropical oceans are potent sources of clean energy. Various countries around the world are investing time and money into the technologies that may tap these renewable power producers, but overcoming the obstacles inherent in these systems will be difficult. The media and industry claim that renewable energies are not yet economically competitive with fossil fuels. Perhaps not, but when one considers the health and environmental costs associated with burning coal and oil, the price of renewable energy becomes more attractive. No renewable energy system will single-handedly replace oil, but together they will become a very important part of the energy mix of the future. Traditional renewable systems are a logical step in the transition to advanced alternative energy sources such as cold fusion. Although scientists and engineers are working feverishly to overcome the various obstacles associated with "new energy" technologies, society should not stand by quietly while researchers wait for a breakthrough. Burning petroleum is polluting our air and water, and the bulk of the world's reserves of cheap oil are concentrated in the politically volatile Persian Gulf. Getting that oil will likely cost billions of dollars and the lives of American soldiers.

Transition to Renewable Energy Needs to Accelerate

Every year Americans consume 25% of all the energy produced in the world, but that conspicuous consumption can't last forever. To that end, the U.S. Department of Energy established the Renewable Energy Production Incentive (REPI) as part of an integrated strategy in the Energy Policy Act of 1992. This act promotes increases in the generation and utilization of electricity from renewable energy sources and furthers the advances of renewable energy technologies. In 1996, the Renewable Energy

Policy Project released "The Environmental Imperative," a plan for the energy market to draw on renewable energy to avoid the severe environmental impacts of the fossil fuel cycle. This plan outlines the environmental imperative for accelerating the use of renewable resources. It is important to realize that it usually takes thirty to forty years to significantly shift fuel patterns and that using electricity as an alternative to oil will require a major adjustment by the American public. The window of opportunity to make this energy transition without a major economic disruption will not be open for long.

8

Renewable Alternatives to Fossil Fuels Are Unnecessary

Thomas Sowell

Thomas Sowell is an economist and a nationally syndicated columnist.

Energy shortages cannot be prevented by transitioning to renewable energy alternatives. Generating alternative energies, including wind and solar power, is too expensive. Energy shortages can be remedied by removing the artificial price controls that cause energy shortages.

As an economist, whenever I hear the word "shortage" I wait for the other shoe to drop. That other shoe is usually "price control." So it was no great surprise to discover, after the electric power shortage in California made headlines, that there were price controls holding down the price of electricity to the consumers.

How Price Controls Work

In the absence of price controls, a shortage is usually a passing thing. When prices are free to rise, that causes consumers to buy less and producers to produce more, eliminating the shortage. But when the price is artificially prevented from rising, the shortage is prevented from ending.

The electric power shortage in California [was] not unique.

What is a new twist, however, is that there are no limits on how much the wholesale electric power suppliers can charge the utility companies that directly supply the consumer.

Since the utility companies have been paying more for electricity than they were allowed to charge their customers, they were operating in the red, and the financial markets are downgrading their bonds. Buying high and selling low is the royal road to bankruptcy, and bonds in a bankrupt company are not usually worth much.

Nor is it any great surprise that "consumer advocates" [denounced] the utilities for seeking a rate increase—or that politicians [proposed] a small increase, completely inadequate to cover the cost of the electricity bought by the utilities. In the never-never land of California ideology, it is considered terrible if the public should have to pay the full cost of what it wants.

> **" Could it possibly be that the costs of generating electricity [using renewables] are higher? "**

In California, prices higher than you like are attributed to "greed" or "gouging" and the answer is either more government regulation or having the government take over the utility company completely and run it. There are people who are old enough to know better who get their 15 minutes of fame by going on television and repeating the sophomoric slogans of their youth, back in the [hippie] days of Berkeley in the 1960s. And there are media people who take them seriously— or at least pretend to.

But just as there is no free lunch, there is no free electricity. And the idea that the government can run businesses at lower costs flies in the face of worldwide evidence that whatever enterprise politicians and bureaucrats run has higher costs. That is why even left-wing governments have been privatizing in recent years, even if this fact has not yet gotten through to those Californians who are still living with the ideological visions of their Berkeley youth.

Far from lowering the cost of producing electricity, government at all levels has for many years and in many ways been needlessly increasing that cost.

Nothing forces prices up like restricting the supply. It has been years since anyone has built more electricity-generating facilities in California because the environmentalists, the courts, the state and local governments and assorted wackos have made it virtually impossible to build a hydroelectric dam, a nuclear power plant or a facility that uses coal or oil to generate electricity.

Renewable Energy Sources Are a Pipe Dream

There are all sorts of bright ideas for generating electricity by using sunlight or windmills. It never seems to occur to those who espouse these ideas to ask why people who have spent a lifetime working in the electricity industry do not share their enthusiasm for these schemes. Could it possibly be that the costs of generating electricity this way are higher?

There are already vast arrays of aging windmills in the hills leading out to California's central valley as monuments to the utopianism that seems to flourish in the Golden State. All that is needed is Don Quixote [writer Miguel de Cervantes' knight who pursued unreachable ideals].

Politics is supposed to be the art of the possible but, in California especially, it is often the art of the impossible. Somehow politicians must make it seem possible to get benefits without paying costs. But if we are too squeamish to build a dam and inconvenience some fish or reptiles, too aesthetically delicate to permit drilling for oil out in the boondocks and too paranoid to allow nuclear power plants to be built, then we should not be surprised if there is not enough electricity to supply our homes and support a growing economy.

The easy answer that is preferred is to use electricity generated outside of California—somewhere out in the real world beyond our borders.

9

Developing Hydrogen Fuel Could Help America Avoid an Energy Crisis

Robert Olson

Robert Olson is the research director for Alternative Futures, a nonprofit research and educational organization founded in 1977.

Global fossil fuel demand is expected to surpass supply at some point over the next few decades. Hydrogen is the best alternative for replacing fossil fuel. Indeed, converting to a hydrogen economy could help the United States avoid an energy crisis. Hydrogen has many benefits as a fuel source; it is reliable and renewable, and because its only emission is pure water, it does not harm the environment. Unfortunately, decades of research and development are still needed for hydrogen to become the new global fuel source.

I t's an exciting time for people involved with hydrogen, but it may also be a dangerous time. With money pouring in for R&D, a flurry of hydrogen workshops and conferences, and increased media attention, the hydrogen field is in the midst of a "bubble" somewhat like the Internet bubble of the 1990s.

Within a year or two, however, it will be clear that some of the business opportunities drawing attention from the private sector aren't as near term as they seemed. Today's overblown claims about how ready the technology is and how fast it can move will be exposed as uninformed. Some people will get disillusioned—and the hydrogen bubble will burst.

What happens then will depend on whether leaders in business and government understand hydrogen's long-term, strategic importance. Without this kind of long-term perspective, hydrogen development could stall.

We need to look beyond the usual planning horizons of business and government to see the enormous long-term benefits of moving toward a more hydrogen-based energy system. These benefits—which justify large, sustained increases in investment—only begin to appear over a decade and can't be fully realized until mid-century or beyond. If leaders appreciate what is possible over a 10- to 50-year period, then when today's hydrogen bubble bursts, it will be possible to settle into more-realistic, steady progress.

Hydrogen's Long-Term Benefits

A substitute for oil. Two-thirds of the 20 million barrels of oil consumed per day in the United States is used for transportation. Hydrogen is the best alternative for replacing that oil, which could be of critical importance sooner than later if gloomy forecasts of oil availability turn out to be right.

Many geologists project that within 10 to 20 years, oil production will no longer be able to keep pace with global demand. Optimistic analysts argue that we will not reach this point until after 2030; pessimists warn that it could happen before this decade is over. Extracting oil from deep-sea regions, tar sands, and oil shale could offset the shortfall for a time, but experts debate how large a role these sources should play because they will be expensive and environmentally damaging.

> *By 2020, the United States will import 70% or more of its oil.*

Given these disagreements and the uncertainties involved, strategic planners at companies such as Royal Dutch Shell and British Petroleum Co. Ltd. are concluding that the time has come to create new corporate divisions devoted to hydrogen as a substitute for oil and to start making major investments.

Security benefits. Even if the peak and decline of global oil production is decades away, developing hydrogen's potential is important for national and global security.

The turmoil in Iraq has once again focused attention on the world's growing dependence on oil from the volatile Persian Gulf region. The United States, for example, imported 54% of its petroleum supply in 2001, almost a quarter of it from the Persian Gulf. By 2020, the United States will import 70% or more of its oil, the U.S. Department of Energy projects. Between now and then, the output of smaller producers will decline and we will become increasingly dependent on a small number of nations with the largest reserves—nations that may include Saudi Arabia, Iraq, Iran, the United Arab Emirates, Kuwait, and Libya.

Given the vital importance of oil to the world economy, the instability of the Persian Gulf region, and hostility toward the United States among populations in the region, this projected level of import dependence should be considered an intolerable security risk. Hydrogen development can reduce that risk because hydrogen can be produced from a wide variety of domestically available resources: natural gas, biomass, wind, hydroelectric, solar, coal, and nuclear.

> *The only emission from fuel cells running on hydrogen is pure water.*

Cost-effective electrical generation. Fuel cells and other micropower sources, collectively called *distributed generation*, will likely emerge as the most economical approach to providing new electrical generating capacity. Micropower on site or feeding a local grid eliminates the cost of distributing power, and in large utility grids most of the cost is actually in transmitting the power rather than in generating it. On-site and local-scale power eliminates grid losses and makes it possible to harness waste heat for heating and cooling.

Environmental benefits. Energy reduction and use is arguably the largest single source of environmental degradation. Environmental impacts include multi-pollutant urban air emissions, regional acid rain, and global warming. By contrast, the only emission from fuel cells running on hydrogen is pure water.

The greatest potential environmental benefits that hydrogen technologies can [offer is to] reduce and eventually eliminate today's massive releases of carbon dioxide from fossil fuel combustion. These emissions are the main driver of global warming.

But how clean hydrogen really is depends on how it is produced. Energy is required to produce elemental hydrogen, and if that energy comes from fossil fuels there will still be emissions, including releases or carbon dioxide. The priority our society gives to minimizing climate change will be a major factor determining what kind of hydrogen economy we create.

Reliable, renewable energy. One of the biggest disadvantages of solar and wind power is their intermittent nature. The sun rises and sets, the wind gusts and calms. Power is not always generated at the times and places where it is needed, and none of today's energy storage technologies is versatile enough to be widely used for storing electricity on a large scale. However, by using renewable energy to produce hydrogen, the hydrogen becomes a storage medium and a "renewable energy carrier" that overcomes these problems.

> *If support for hydrogen falters, hydrogen would not be ready as a substitute for oil once global oil demand exceeds supply.*

Renewable energy technologies, like hydrogen itself, will take decades to put into place on a large scale. In the near term, the cheapest way to produce hydrogen is by reforming natural gas. Because natural gas is the cleanest fossil fuel, it is likely to play a major transitional role even if renewable energy technologies eventually come to dominate electricity and hydrogen production.

Sustainable global development. Today's industrial nations were able to base their development on cheap oil. That option is unlikely to remain available for very long to the world's developing nations. Oil will become more expensive over the decades ahead and global warming may force us to move away from oil long before reserves are depleted. Hydrogen technologies can allow developing nations to move toward U.S. and European levels of affluence without depleting resources or compromising the environment.

Achieving this vision will require further progress and cost reduction in hydrogen production, storage, distribution, and conversion. But no technological show stoppers appear to stand in the way. Hydrogen produced from a wide variety of sources, and ultimately perhaps from just sunlight and water, should be able to sustain economic activity and personal mobility indefinitely.

How Things Could Go Wrong:
Three Negative Scenarios

Unfortunately, there is a very real possibility that society will fail to achieve many of these benefits. The three negative scenarios below illustrate how things could go wrong.

Negative Scenario 1: Faltering Support. When today's exaggerated expectations are not realized, political support for hydrogen may falter. Government budget cuts could be crippling to companies that have invested heavily in hydrogen R&D with hopes of profits down the road. Some of the most innovative companies are already struggling in the current climate of economic uncertainty and falling stock prices.

Ironically, the chances that hydrogen will lose political support are increased by some of the United States' own efforts to promote it. Increased R&D funding to develop hydrogen fuel cell cars over the long run was accompanied by an abandonment of R&D aimed at making cars cleaner and more fuel-efficient in the short run. Some environmental groups thus denounced hydrogen R&D programs as a "dirty energy plan" because much of the research is focused on ways to produce hydrogen from gasoline, coal, and nuclear power.

Environmentalists could be further angered if expanding fuel cell production produces new pollution and waste-disposal problems. So far, little attention has been given to applying "design for the environment" principles to fuel cell manufacturing in order to design out environmental problems early on. Political and consumer support for hydrogen could also weaken if accidents involving hydrogen begin to make the headlines.

If support for hydrogen falters, hydrogen would not be ready as a substitute for oil once global oil demand exceeds supply. Oil prices would increase and might reach levels that trigger a global energy crisis with severe, long-term economic impacts.

Negative Scenario 2: Premature Lock-In. Another way hydrogen development could go wrong is through a premature commitment to technologies that could soon be supplanted by better ones. Developing markets sometimes lock in early on inferior designs, as happened when the awkward QWERTY keyboard format achieved a virtual monopoly, or when VHS achieved dominance over Betamax in the VCR market.

> // As demand for hydrogen grows, the central question of hydrogen development will be how best to produce it. //

There are several ways this kind of premature lock-in could happen in hydrogen development. The most hotly debated possibility involves the question of whether an initial generation of hydrogen fuel cell cars should be designed to run on gasoline. Several oil companies and automobile manufacturers have favored this approach and it has benefited from heavy government R&D support. It involves building cars with onboard fuel processors to reform gasoline to hydrogen. The great advantage of this strategy is that it allows fuel cell cars to piggyback on the existing gasoline production and distribution infrastructure, avoiding the time and financial risks involved in building a new hydrogen infrastructure. It could allow fuel cell cars to come into the market sooner than would otherwise be possible.

Critics argue that this attempt to make a fast start on fuel cell cars will slow investment in creating a hydrogen infrastructure, causing a false start for the hydrogen transition as a whole. They point to studies suggesting that cars using onboard fuel processors are likely to be expensive and inefficient with no advantages over fuel-electric hybrids. If fuel cells and reformers are too expensive, they are likely to fail in the marketplace and give fuel cell cars a bad reputation.

On the other hand, critics worry that if cars with onboard fuel processors do succeed in the marketplace, the auto market could lock-in on them for decades, denying society the benefits of more-advanced cars that ran directly on hydrogen. Direct hydrogen vehicles would cut dependence on imported oil, improve vehicle energy efficiency, and completely eliminate exhaust and carbon-dioxide emissions. Most importantly, using direct hydrogen would decouple energy sources from the vehicles themselves, giving vehicles the flexibility to run on hydrogen produced from a variety of domestic resources.

Negative Scenario 3: Undesirable Hydrogen Infrastructures. There are many ways in which a hydrogen infrastructure with highly undesirable consequences might be created. Suppose, for example, that hydrogen development focuses on reforming hydrogen from natural gas and coal. This could happen if renewable energy (solar, wind) is never able to compete effectively against heavily subsidized fossil fuels and if nuclear power remains blocked by investor wariness and public opposition. Suppose, further, that technologies for capturing and sequestering the carbon dioxide produced in reforming natural gas and coal prove too expensive for widespread use. Then hydrogen development might make it possible to move away from oil toward gas and coal—but growing carbon-dioxide emission would continue to drive global warming.

Another potential problem: Public demand for sharp reductions in fossil-fuel burning could open the door to a global revival of nuclear power. This kind of shift in public opinion is possible if, as many climate models predict, the next few decades bring higher sea levels, more extreme weather events, and costly impacts on water resources, coastal development, and agriculture. Nuclear energy is the one mature technology able to produce both hydrogen and electricity with no greenhouse-gas emissions.

But deploying nuclear power globally on a massive scale would take us toward a future where tens of thousands of bombs' worth of nuclear materials are being produced, enriched, reprocessed, and shipped around the world every year. Given the growing dangers of nuclear proliferation and terrorism, is that a future we really want to create?

If Things Go Right: Four Positive Scenarios

Positive Scenario 1: Full Spectrum Development. One route to a positive future involves continuing to provide R&D support for fuel cells, but focusing less on using them in cars and more on using them for generating electricity. This is a sensible business strategy because fuel cells will move into power-generation markets over the years just ahead, but fuel cell costs will need to drop considerably to be viable for widespread use in cars. That will probably take 15 years or more.

Developing large-scale fuel cell manufacturing operations for power markets is the best strategy for bringing fuel cell costs down to where they become practical for use in cars. While power markets are being developed, automobile manufacturers could follow a path being pioneered by BMW and Ford and produce internal combustion engines modified to run on hydrogen. Although not pollution free, these engines have much lower emissions than conventional gasoline engines and require no major retooling in the auto industry. This approach would quickly increase the demand for hydrogen, accelerating the development of a hydrogen infrastructure.

> *Developing the full spectrum of potential hydrogen sources keeps options open and elicits support from all parts of the energy industry.*

As demand for hydrogen grows, the central question of hydrogen development will be how best to produce it. Reforming hydrogen from natural gas is the most economical option now and will be for some time, but governments and energy companies are already beginning to invest in developing more cost-effective ways to produce hydrogen from biomass, coal, nuclear power, solar, and other forms of renewable energy. Developing the full spectrum of potential hydrogen sources keeps options open and elicits support from all parts of the energy industry. Parallel investments in methods to capture and sequester carbon dioxide are essential in this kind of scenario so that the full range of fossil fuel sources can be used in a climatically benign way.

The major risk in this approach is making investments for political reasons rather than on the basis of objective assessments. Newer hydrogen production options using renewable energy could get less financial support than those championed by powerful, mature industries like oil, coal, and nuclear.

Positive Scenario 2: Solar Hydrogen. Many people involved in hydrogen believe the long-term "home run" of hydrogen development would be an energy-efficient economy based on hydrogen extracted from water using solar energy. They think that if this kind of hydrogen development path proves possible it would be best for the environment, best for national and global security, and best for sustainable global development.

The hope is that a solar hydrogen future will emerge from a full spectrum development approach when objective assessments of the full costs and benefits of different options guide investments. Wind power is already becoming competitive with coal. Solar electricity costs will fall sharply over the next few years as thin-film materials replace rigid silicon disks in photovoltaic systems. Major corporations like General Electric and BP are investing heavily in wind and wind and photovoltaic systems with an eye not only to markets in industrial nations but also to the 2 billion people in developing countries without electric power. And a number of the entrepreneurs and venture capitalists who made fortunes in the high-tech boom of the 1990s are now convinced that renewable energy combined with hydrogen, is "the next big thing"—a disruptive technology that will transform entire industries.

A solar hydrogen economy is much more likely to emerge if governments help drive demand and spur innovation. The state-level practice of setting goals for energy generation from renewable sources could spread throughout the United States. Government-organized markets for trading in carbon would promote investment in energy efficiency as well as renewable energy. Well targeted increases in R&D funding could spur progress in critical areas such as improving the efficiency of photovoltaic cells and reducing the cost of electrolyzers for hydrogen production.

> *Technological developments outside the hydrogen field could actually enhance hydrogen's promise.*

The danger in this approach is that solar technologies may not perform as well technically and economically as their proponents hope. That concern justifies keeping other hydrogen production options open, even if solar hydrogen looks increasingly attractive.

Positive Scenario 3: Apollo Project for Hydrogen. Senator Byron Dorgan (Democrat, North Dakota) wants "an Apollo-type initiative" and has introduced legislation supporting a $6.5 billion, 10-year plan. However, an effort really equivalent to the Apollo project would mean spending about $100 billion in today's dollars over a decade. Yet given the full range of hydrogen's benefits—liberating the United States from oil dependence, preserving personal mobility, reducing air pollution, stemming global warming, and providing a foundation for sustainable global development—can it be argued that investment on this scale is not worthwhile?

What makes an effort this large plausible is that most of the technical challenges involved only require engineering improvements, not scientific breakthroughs. That means spending more money can bring faster progress.

What makes an effort like this problematic is the difficulty of making wise investments quickly when we still lack agreement on the best technical path forward. A slower effort, on a similar scale, with more pilot projects, more careful assessments of benefits and costs, and more opportunities to test alternative approaches in the marketplace might bring better results.

> *New options are likely to become available for producing hydrogen.*

Positive Scenario 4: Technology Transformation. Technological developments outside the hydrogen field could actually enhance hydrogen's promise. For example, progress in the development of nanomaterials could lead to improved membranes and catalysts that make fuel cells cheaper and more efficient. Nanomaterials could also revolutionize hydrogen storage, making it possible to produce advanced hydrogen absorbents and strong, lightweight tanks to safely store highly compressed gas. Tiny embedded sensors for detecting stresses and leaks could improve hydrogen safety. Nanorod solar cells made from electrically conductive polymers shot through with nanoscale semiconducting crystals could prove as efficient as the best of the old silicon-based solar cells, but dirt cheap. They could be rolled out like plastic wrap, ink-jet printed, or even painted onto surfaces.

New options are likely to become available for producing hydrogen. Photoelectrochemical-based water-splitting systems could produce hydrogen directly from sunlight and water. Biological dissemblers could replace older technologies for extracting hydrogen from biomass wastes. Bioreactors could produce hydrogen using bacteria and algae that have been modified chemically, physiologically, and genetically to maximum production efficiency.

Looking back from 2030 at the polluting, resource-depleting, and nuclear proliferation–prone energy systems of the late twentieth century, people may find it hard to imagine how anyone could have seriously believed that these were "advanced technologies."

Strategic Conversations About Hydrogen

Scenarios like these could be developed more systematically, and there are other images of the hydrogen future that are equally plausible, yet the actual future is unlikely to be exactly like any of them. Scenarios don't predict the future; they are merely tools for thinking more clearly and creatively in situations where the future is unpredictable. Good scenarios provide an intellectual framework and a common vocabulary for strategic conversations.

Business and government leaders involved in hydrogen development need to engage in strategic conversations about the long-term big picture of alternative paths and key choices ahead. Among the questions these leaders should tackle: What are the different plausible scenarios of pathways toward a hydrogen future? How can we assess which paths are likely to be least expensive, best for the environment, and most adaptive to technological change? What can business and government do to avoid locking in prematurely on technologies and paths forward that could soon be supplanted by better ones? Without exploring questions like those and assessing the pros and cons of a wide range of scenarios, we might create a hydrogen future that fails to give us many of the benefits that make hydrogen so attractive.

The key to moving beyond today's hydrogen bubble is to develop a widely shared long-term perspective on the enormous benefits that hydrogen development can provide. And the key to achieving those benefits is to develop a long-term perspective on the alternative paths ahead and the kind of future we really want to create.

10

Nuclear Power Could Help Avert a World Energy Crisis

John J. Taylor

John J. Taylor, retired vice president for nuclear power at the Electric Power Research Institute, is a consultant to the Center for Global Security Research in Livermore, California.

The expansion of nuclear power has virtually reached a standstill. However, as future global power needs expand at a steady rate and fossil fuel sources become more and more scarce, the nuclear power industry must expand. For this to happen, public trust must first be earned by establishing a credible safety record. As fossil fuel prices rise and capital costs of nuclear plants decrease, nuclear power will become more economically competitive and thus a viable and pollution-free substitute for global energy needs.

President Dwight D. Eisenhower electrified the United Nations (UN) General Assembly with his vision that "the fearful trend of atomic military buildup can be reversed, this greatest destructive force can be developed into a great boon for the benefit of all mankind . . . to serve the peaceful pursuits of mankind . . . [in] electrical energy, agriculture, medicine, and other peaceful activities." He further proposed to "allocate fissionable material [for peaceful uses] from a bank under international atomic energy agency control [and] . . . provide special safe conditions under which such a bank of fissionable material can be

John J. Taylor, "The Nuclear Power Bargain," *Issues in Science and Technology*, vol. 20, Spring 2004. Copyright © 2004 by the University of Texas at Dallas, Richardson, TX. Reproduced by permission.

made essentially immune to surprise seizure." Although the "bank" never eventuated, the Nuclear Non-Proliferation Treaty (NPT) and the International Atomic Energy Agency (IAEA) were instituted to apply the controls associated with a new "bargain": Nations forgoing nuclear weapons development would be given the peaceful benefits of nuclear technology.

> *Expansion of nuclear power has reached a virtual standstill.*

The initiatives stemming from Eisenhower's 1953 address helped quite literally to electrify the world. Today, 441 nuclear power plants provide 16 percent of the world's electricity. After years of intensive technical and institutional development to correct early problems, these plants are now operating safely and, on average, with high reliability and competitive costs. Many countries depend critically on nuclear power. Among the 10 countries that rely on it most heavily (Lithuania, France, Belgium, Slovakia, Bulgaria, Ukraine, Sweden, Slovenia, Armenia, and Switzerland), nuclear power provides some 40 to 80 percent of each nation's electricity. Not far behind are the Republic of Korea (38 percent) and Japan (35 percent). The United States, at 20 percent, ranks 19th but generates more electricity from nuclear plants than any other country, and six of its states derive 50 percent or more of their electricity from nuclear power. As licenses of existing U.S. plants are being extended by 20 years, and as similar actions are taken overseas, continued usage at present levels through mid-century seems assured.

Unclear Future for Nuclear Power

What is less clear is whether nuclear power capacity will actually expand during that period. Certainly the potential is there. Major growth in primary energy production will be needed to serve a global population that could reach 9 or 10 billion by 2100. Electricity demand is projected to grow by 480 percent in a high economic scenario and by up to 140 percent in an ecologically driven scenario governed by conservation and the reduction of greenhouse gas emissions. Given those looming needs, it seems logical to predict a widening role for a source of economical combustion-free energy that does not generate greenhouse gas or air pollution emissions and that uses a fuel supply that is sustainable over the long haul.

But expansion of nuclear power has reached a virtual standstill. In the United States, no orders have been placed for nuclear power plants in more than two decades. Worldwide, only 32 nuclear power plants are under construction, most of them in India and China. From the mid-1980s until recently, R & D budgets for civilian power had been steadily declining in most of the industrialized countries, with the exception of Japan and France. The downturn is largely a result of slower growth in electricity demand and an abundance of natural gas at low prices. Under those conditions, gas-fired plants have grown more economical for expanding capacity. But history also plays a role. The legacy of earlier problems, including the high-profile accidents at Three Mile Island and Chernobyl, remains in the form of continued public skepticism about the safety of nuclear power and its radioactive wastes. Those concerns are amplified by a general fear of radiation and the specter of the atom bomb. In response, Sweden, Italy, and Germany have imposed moratoriums on nuclear power.

> *A significant increase in the price of natural gas could make new nuclear plants economically competitive even without further reductions in their capital costs.*

To contribute significantly to global energy demand, the nuclear power industry must earn public confidence by maintaining an excellent safety record. But success in the marketplace depends on economic factors: the capital cost of new plants and the operating and maintenance costs of existing and new plants. These costs are strongly influenced by safety, reliability, environmental considerations (global climate change, regional air pollution, and waste disposition), and the adequacy and stability of fuel supply. Research, development, and demonstration (RD & D), for both the near and long terms, are necessary to meet this total cost challenge, as well as to achieve advanced system performance. Nuclear plants' resistance to proliferation must also be addressed. Revelations that some countries have developed weapons capabilities clandestinely, using nuclear power development as a cover, point up serious weaknesses in the international proliferation control system.

All of these issues are being dealt with to varying degrees, but considerably more progress will be needed before Eisenhower's vision for peaceful uses of nuclear energy can be fully realized.

A History of Nuclear Power

In its early decades, nuclear power became a victim of its own success. It grew as an energy source at about three times the rate of previous new sources of electricity generation. Partly because of that rapid expansion, a series of problems emerged. U.S. plant reliability deteriorated: The average capacity factor (the ratio of energy produced to the amount of energy that could have been generated at continuous full-power operation) fell to 60 percent versus the 80 percent expected. Because of a lack of timely and in-depth planning for the disposition of radioactive waste, efforts to develop a high-level waste repository were making little progress. The safety regulatory base was immature. As nuclear power developed, contractors faced major delays in gaining construction permits and were forced to undertake substantial retrofitting of plants under construction and already completed.

Then in 1979, the Three Mile Island accident occurred, partially melting that plant's fuel and causing multibillion dollar losses in the plant investment and in the cost of cleanup and decommissioning. Because the plant was enclosed in a reinforced concrete "containment" to keep radiation from escaping, neither the public nor the plant operators were harmed. But many design, operational, and maintenance deficiencies were revealed that required years of technical and management remediation and significantly increased safety regulatory requirements.

The development of more rigorous operational standards since the Three Mile Island accident has had a salutary effect on the nuclear power industry. The Institute for Nuclear Power Operations was formed in the United States to establish standards of operational excellence and to monitor compliance with those standards by all U.S. commercial nuclear power plants. Later, in the wake of the lethal accident of the uncontained Chernobyl nuclear plant in Ukraine, this concept was expanded internationally with the formation of the World Association of Nuclear Operators.

These reforms have led to excellent safety and reliability records. U.S. plants posted average capacity factors of 91.5 percent in 2001, 91.7 percent in 2002, and 89.4 percent in 2003. The increased average capacity factor since 1992 is roughly equivalent to 13 new 1,000-megawatt (MW) plants. Parallel improvements were achieved worldwide, though with less difficulty than in the United States. In Western Europe and Asia, rapid expansion was made possible primarily by technology transfer of light water reactor (LWR) technology from the United States. Those plants proved more reliable initially than the older technology that produces the bulk of U.S. nuclear power, in part because they were deployed somewhat later and benefited from the early U.S. experience. Worldwide, nuclear plants in 2003 achieved an average capacity factor of 80 percent and 87.3 percent average availability (that is, ready to provide power but not called on by the grid).

The Current State of Nuclear Power

Thanks to improvements derived from operational experience and innovative reactor technologies, prospects have recently been enhanced for deploying new nuclear plants in the near term in the United States, Europe, and Asia that will be even safer and more reliable. Advanced light water reactors (ALWRs) have been developed in a program managed by the Electric Power Research Institute (EPRI) and cost-shared by the U.S. Department of Energy (DOE), U.S. reactor manufacturers, and utilities in the United States, Europe, and Asia.

ALWRs in the power range of 1,000 to 1,200 MW have been developed that derive their improved design and operational features from extensive worldwide licensing and operating experience with LWR systems. A 600-MW ALWR incorporating innovative passive (gravity and pressurized gas) emergency core and containment cooling systems has also been developed. These passive systems replace the electrically or steam-powered pumping systems used in the conventional plants, resulting in a simpler and less costly design.

Four 1,350-MW ALWRs of the boiling water type (ABWRs), designed jointly by General Electric (GE) and Hitachi/Toshiba, have already been built in Japan. Two more are under construction in Taiwan. South Korea is also building four Westinghouse 1,000-MW ALWR plants of the pressurized water type (APWR).

All of these designs have been certified by the U.S. Nuclear Regulatory Commission (NRC). The NRC has also certified a 600-MW passively cooled APWR, the Westinghouse AP-600, after extensive tests of its passive cooling features. China has continued to expand its nuclear power capacity, and is presently building two more 1,000-MW APWRs under French contracts. Finland has awarded a contract to Framatome/Siemens to build a 1,600-MW APWR. France is nearing a decision on whether to authorize a 1,600-MW plant of the same design.

The Economic Competitiveness of Nuclear Power

Because of their relatively high capital cost, these plants do not yet compete economically with fossil power, at least in the United States. Consequently, efforts are under way to further reduce their capital cost. Westinghouse has developed the AP-1000, a 1,000-MW version of its AP-600 that could reach economic competitiveness through economy of scale. It is now being reviewed for an NRC design certification. GE is developing a 1,350-MW passively cooled ABWR, the ESBWR, with similar economic promise, and has applied for NRC design certification.

Nuclear power has a clear environmental edge, helping to lower average emissions from the power industry overall.

A significant increase in the price of natural gas could make new nuclear plants economically competitive even without further reductions in their capital costs. The competitive position of the combined-cycle gas-fired turbine (CCGT) power plant, the type most favored for new generation capacity over the past two decades, is highly sensitive to the price of gas. For most of this period, gas prices have been in the range of $3 to $4 per million British thermal units (MMBTU). At those rates, the overnight capital cost (the cost excluding interest on capital) of a new nuclear plant would need to be in the range of $1,000 per kilowatt (kW) to be competitive, which is the cost goal of the AP-1000 and the ESBWR. But if gas remains at its current price of $5 to $6 per MMBTU, a competitive nuclear plant overnight capital cost could be as high as $1,300 to $1,400 per kW, the present estimate for the conventionally cooled ABWR.

> *Increased nuclear fuel resources are achieved by producing more plutonium during operation and thus creating more fuel than is burned.*

These cost comparisons focus on gas-fired plants because the CCGT has been the technology of choice for new capacity. If gas prices remain high, coal-fired plants could become the prime competitor with nuclear plants. In that case, nuclear power might prevail, partly because the present cost gap is smaller and partly because of another important part of the energy equation: environmental costs.

The Environmental Costs of Nuclear Power

The environmental costs of nuclear power are internalized; that is, they are largely included in the cost of construction, operation, and insurance and are added to the price of electricity. That is not the case with fossil fuel plants. The market does not currently reward nuclear power's environmental benefits nor have the environmental costs from fossil fuel plants been fully internalized. And yet nuclear power has a clear environmental edge, helping to lower average emissions from the power industry overall. Between 1973 and 2001, U.S. power plants emitted 70.3 million fewer tons of sulfur dioxide, 35.6 million fewer tons of nitrogen oxides, and 2.97 billion fewer tons of carbon dioxide than if nuclear power had not been part of the energy mix. Without major deployment of nuclear energy and noncombustible renewables, the world's total carbon dioxide emissions from power generation are expected to grow from 23 billion tons in 1990 to 40 billion tons in 2020. For the time being, the avoidance of greenhouse gas emissions through nuclear power has not been recognized in the Clean Development Mechanism of the UN Framework Convention on Climate Change as one of the methods allowed for achieving the required reduction. Nor are nuclear plants eligible for emissions trading to gain financial credit for their contribution to reduced air pollution and greenhouse gas emissions.

But that could change. If the costs of greenhouse gas emissions from fossil fuel plants are internalized (say, if the plants are required to build carbon separation and sequestration systems or to pay a carbon tax) or if emissions trading is granted to nuclear plants, the economic tables would be turned. Add to that the financial risk arising from the greater fuel supply and cost instabilities of fossil fuel plants, and it becomes apparent that nuclear power might be on the threshold of achieving economic competitiveness.

Managing Nuclear Waste

Another issue that must be cleared up to allow a sustained expansion of nuclear power is the disposition of spent fuel, virtually all of which is currently stored at the nuclear power plant sites. Progress is being made, albeit slowly, toward the implementation of permanent repositories. In the United States, Congress has authorized DOE to proceed with the licensing of a permanent repository at Yucca Mountain in Nevada. The site is proposed for the disposition of some 70,000 tons of used fuel, which is sufficient for the 40,000-plus tons produced to date and for some 20 years to come. The authorization was based on more than 10 years of intensive R & D and engineering studies. If a construction license is granted, DOE will begin construction in early 2008. Before completion, DOE will update its application for a license to receive and possess waste, as required by NRC regulations. If that license is granted, waste could begin arriving as early as 2010.

> **//** *Nuclear power plants are now being used to reduce proliferation risk.* **//**

Other countries are also making progress in radioactive waste management. Sweden has put into operation an efficient repository of adequate capacity for its low-level nuclear plant wastes and has begun the design and licensing of an intermediate-level waste repository. Finland has adequate storage capacity for its low-level wastes, and a spent-fuel repository is being designed and licensed. France has decided to build two underground laboratories for research on spent-fuel disposition, one in clay and one in granite. Most other countries are at an earlier stage.

The security of nuclear facilities against attack has been addressed urgently ever since [the September 11, 2001, terrorist attacks]. Initial evaluations suggest that nuclear power plants with containment (all except some in Russia), fuel storage facilities, and transport casks are robust against such attack. Nevertheless, plant security has been substantially bolstered. The NRC is expanding safety regulations to include the possibility of attacks on nuclear plants, both by increasing security requirements and by defining a "design basis threat" on which every nuclear plant must be evaluated. Other nations are making similar evaluations.

One obstacle to expanded nuclear power is licensing uncertainty. In the United States, changes in licensing requirements after the start of construction and delays in getting the operating permit after completion have in the past greatly increased capital costs and construction time. To cope with this problem, the NRC established a licensing standardization policy that allows a reactor manufacturer to seek a site-independent design certification and a prospective plant owner/operator to obtain a separate early site permit. With a certified design and an early site permit, a combined construction and operating permit can be obtained before any money is invested in plant equipment and construction.

In light of all these developments, the prospects for recommencing new construction in the United States are fairly strong. Congress has authorized a joint cost-shared DOE/industry program called the Nuclear Power 2010 Initiative, which aims to begin building new nuclear plants in the United States around 2010. The planning framework is contained in DOE's Near Term Deployment Roadmap. First priority is being given to resolving critical issues such as competitive costs and to defining the private-sector financing mechanisms.

New Uses for Nuclear Power

Near-term deployment of new nuclear plants will strengthen the resource and skill base in the nuclear industry, providing a foundation on which more advanced designs and a broader scope of power applications can be developed. Nuclear energy is presented with four major future opportunities, each requiring major long-term RD & D:

- Expanding the end uses of nuclear electricity for tasks such as powering electrical vehicles and providing high-temperature heat for industrial processes.
- Developing economical hydrogen fuel production and desalination using nuclear energy to provide inexpensive bulk power.
- Building nuclear plants that run on reprocessed spent fuel, which will ensure that the fuel supply will be adequate for centuries.
- Developing economical small-output nuclear plants that could provide the benefits of nuclear power to smaller and less developed countries.

DOE has launched a pair of efforts—the Generation IV Program and the Advanced Fuel Cycle Initiative (AFCI)—to carry out the RD & D to realize those four opportunities while achieving economic competitiveness, high standards of safety and proliferation resistance, and effective waste management. The Generation IV Program has chosen for initial study six different reactor concepts for development: gas-cooled, sodium-cooled, lead-cooled, molten salt-cooled, supercritical water-cooled, and very-high-temperature gas-cooled. All would operate at high temperatures to achieve greater efficiency. The very-high-temperature gas-cooled reactor has the potential to be an efficient hydrogen producer to provide fuel for the transportation sector so as to reduce dependence on offshore oil.

International cooperation is being fostered through the Generation IV International Forum, which includes representatives from 10 countries (Argentina, Brazil, Canada, France, Japan, the Republic of South Africa, the Republic of Korea, Switzerland, the United Kingdom, and the United States), and through the IAEA's advanced reactor development program (INPRO).

Uranium Supply for Nuclear Power

An expanded long-term reliance on nuclear power is possible only if uranium supplies are adequate. Assuming a modest growth rate for nuclear power of 2 percent per year until 2050, and assuming continued operation without fuel recycling, annual uranium requirements would grow by a factor of about three, to roughly 200,000 tons. The cumulative uranium requirement from now to 2050 would exceed 5 million tons. The IAEA and the Organisation for Economic Co-Operation and Development estimate that some 4 million tons of uranium would be available at costs of up to $130 per kilogram (about twice current prices), resulting in a deficit of roughly 1 million tons of natural uranium by 2050. A major goal of the AFCI is to close this gap by developing proliferation-resistant fuel recycling for one or more of the Generation IV concepts. Success in these technologies could expand nuclear fuel resources a hundredfold.

> *Another defense against proliferation is the concept of regional fuel services.*

A variety of fuel cycles are under consideration, including plutonium and thorium recycling in conventional LWRs and in advanced fast-spectrum reactors. Advanced aqueous and innovative pyrometallurgical reprocessing options are being pursued. Increased nuclear fuel resources are achieved by producing more plutonium during operation and thus creating more fuel than is burned. Alternatively, thorium fuels can be used to produce fissionable uranium-233. The goal for all variants is to retain the actinides in the reprocessed fuel so as to eliminate the potential for diversion of fissionable material from the waste stream and to minimize its long-lived radioactivity content.

A nuclear power electric generator of small nominal output can extend the benefits of nuclear technology to small developing nations. To achieve cost competitiveness through economy of scale, present nuclear plants are in the range of 1,000 to 1,500 MW. But the grid capacity of many of the developing countries is too small to justify such a large single block of power. The Generation IV Program is pursuing the concept of small, integrated, transportable lead alloy—cooled power packages in the 100-MW range that do not require refueling and could provide power over a 10-year period. A key goal is to ensure that these plants are highly resistant to proliferation.

Both the Generation IV Program and the Nuclear Power 2010 Initiative are receiving an infusion of ideas from DOE's Nuclear Energy Research Initiative (NERI), which fosters innovative R & D on advanced nuclear energy concepts and technologies. NERI recently completed the first round of 46 research projects initiated in fiscal year 1999. The effort marshals the talents of more than 250 U.S. university students and includes collaborations with more than 25 international organizations.

Proliferation Resistance

Although there has been no known diversion of weapons-usable nuclear material from safeguarded civilian facilities since the inception of the IAEA, among the problems still facing nuclear power is the need to boost resistance to proliferation. In fact, nuclear power plants are now being used to reduce proliferation risk: The potential for diversion of highly enriched uranium (HEU) and plutonium declared excess under the U.S.-Russian START [Strategic Arms Reduction Treaty] nuclear arms reduction agreements. These excess weapons materials are being disposed of by converting them to fuel for electricity generation in U.S. nuclear plants. About one-third of the Russian HEU stockpile has already been processed, permanently disposing of the weapons material from 6,000 nuclear warheads.

Yet the fact that nuclear power development has been used as a cover for nuclear weapons development is cause for concern. NPT signatories need to be prevented from engaging in any such deceptions. The most critical need is to put teeth into NPT enforcement through the UN Security Council or through a separate entity such as the one evolving under the multilateral Proliferation Security Initiative. Other urgent needs are to upgrade export controls and materials inventory and to strengthen IAEA inspection and monitoring of NPT compliance. . . .

What is certain is the urgent need, in the words of Eisenhower, to turn "this greatest destructive force . . . into a great boon for the benefit of all mankind.

Beyond institutional measures, the plants themselves should incorporate improved design features that render them inherently more resistant to proliferation. Improved analytical assessments should be conducted to identify the points at which nuclear power plants and related facilities are most vulnerable and to suggest design remedies. Possible approaches include making weapons-usable materials less accessible; erecting chemical, physical and radiation barriers; limiting the ability of an enrichment facility to produce weapons-usable material; and increasing the time required to effect a diversion. If intrinsic design features were improved, the institutional tasks of surveillance, monitoring, inspection, accountability, and physical security would also become easier. Such analyses could determine the proper balance between intrinsic features and institutional control processes. An outline of the overall assessment process, the R & D necessary to develop it, and potential intrinsic proliferation-resistant features is contained in the DOE report, Technology Opportunities to Increase the Proliferation Resistance of Civilian Nuclear Power Systems.

Regional Fuel Services

Another defense against proliferation is the concept of regional fuel services. Although the Eisenhower proposal for an international bank of fissionable material never materialized, the idea has merit as a means of handling those portions of the nuclear fuel cycle that are of primary concern from a proliferation standpoint: uranium enrichment and plutonium separation. If countries interested in developing nuclear power were provided such services, there would be no reason for them to invest in fuel-processing facilities that could be used to divert weapons-usable materials.

Both government and private organizations could provide such services under strict regulation, with complete transparency, and with unconstrained access for compliance monitoring. They would need to meet high standards of accreditation and have a record of compliance with the NPT. Contractual arrangements for these services would have to ensure a steady fuel supply. Large commercial facilities now provide such fuel services globally, and they could continue to do so upon accreditation under the stricter international nonproliferation regime that will be needed for the future.

The regional/international services concept could also be extended to the storage and disposition of spent fuel and high-level waste. Presently, individual nations carry these responsibilities. Although the IAEA sets international standards, they are followed at the discretion of each country. For many countries, high cost, political opposition, and a limited number of qualified sites make the development of geological repositories very difficult. Another concern is that spent fuel repositories will become less resistant to proliferation once their radiation levels have decayed for a century or so. For these reasons, cooperative regional repositories will become appropriate to provide a broad base of support for protecting these facilities.

Recently, several proposals have been made to create international spent fuel storage facilities and repositories, as well as fuel-processing facilities. In each scheme, the IAEA would be the authority responsible for verifying adherence to stringent safeguards and ensuring the transparency and accountability of related activities. Bringing such a plan to fruition will not be easy, but it should be made a goal for a continued Atoms for Peace vision.

Realizing Eisenhower's Vision for Nuclear Power

There are strong reasons to believe that Eisenhower's vision of serving "the peaceful pursuits of mankind" through nuclear energy can be more fully realized in the years ahead. The enormous projected growth in electricity demand to serve a greatly expanded global population and to redress the economic imbalance among nations makes clear the need. Nuclear energy, which produces essentially no air pollution or greenhouse gas emissions, can help to meet that need and be put to other peaceful uses if economic competitiveness can be achieved.

Recent proliferation challenges by rogue states and terrorism make Eisenhower's call "to reverse the atomic military buildup" as relevant today as it was 50 years ago. The NPT, the IAEA, and the cooperation of many nations have helped stem that buildup. With the support of the UN Security Council, they could go on to remedy the current inadequacies in the international nonproliferation regime.

These actions are needed to address the weaknesses on both sides of the nuclear "bargain." They must be supplemented by greater public acceptance of nuclear power—acceptance that can be gained only through an excellent record of safety and reliability and through open communication with the public about the benefits and the risks of nuclear power. The tasks are not easy and the outcomes not certain. What is certain is the urgent need, in the words of Eisenhower, to turn "this greatest destructive force . . . into a great boon for the benefit of all mankind."

Organizations to Contact

The editors have compiled the following list of organizations concerned with the issues debated in this book. The descriptions are derived from materials provided by the organizations. All have publications or information available for interested readers. The list was compiled on the date of publication of the present volume; names, addresses, phone and fax numbers, and e-mail addresses may change. Be aware that many organizations take several weeks or longer to respond to inquiries, so allow as much time as possible.

American Petroleum Institute (API)
1220 L St. NW, Washington, DC 20005
(202) 682-8000
Web site: www.api.org

As the primary trade association of the oil and natural gas industry, API represents more than four hundred members involved in all aspects of the oil and natural gas industry. This organization offers a variety of information about energy on its Web site.

American Solar Energy Society (ASES)
2400 Central Ave., Suite A, Boulder, CO 80301
(303) 443-3130
Web site: www.ases.org

ASES promotes the widespread near-term and long-term use of solar energy. It organizes the National Solar Energy Conference, the National Solar Tour, and publishes *Solar Today* magazine.

American Wind Energy Association (AWEA)
1101 Fourteenth St. NW, 12th Fl., Washington, DC 20005
(202) 383-2500 • fax: (202) 383-2505
Web site: www.awea.org

Since 1974 the AWEA has advocated the development of wind energy as a reliable, environmentally superior energy alternative in the United States and around the world. Publications include the *AWEA Wind Energy Weekly* and the monthly *Windletter.*

Council on Alternative Fuels (CAF)
1225 I St. NW, Suite 320, Washington, DC 20005
(202) 898-0711

CAF is comprised of companies interested in the production of synthetic fuels and the research and development of synthetic fuel technology. It publishes information on new alternative fuels in the monthly *Alternative Fuel News.*

Geothermal Education Office (GEO)
664 Hilary Dr., Tiburon, CA 94920
(415) 435-4574 • (800) 866-4436
Web site: http://geothermal.marin.org

GEO produces and distributes educational materials about geothermal energy to schools, energy and environmental educators, libraries, industry, and the public. GEO collaborates frequently with education and energy organizations with common goals, and, through its Web site, responds to requests and questions from around the world.

Geothermal Resources Council (GRC)
PO Box 1350, Davis, CA 95617-1350
(530) 758-2360 • fax: (530) 758-2839
Web site: www.geothermal.org

The GRC encourages the development of geothermal resources worldwide through the collection and timely distribution of data and technological information. It also serves as a public forum for the world geothermal community, and provides transfer of objective and unbiased information on the nature of geothermal energy and its development.

International Association for Hydrogen Energy (IAHE)
PO Box 248266, Coral Gables, FL 33124
e-mail: ayfer@iahe.org • Web site: www.iahe.org

The IAHE strives to advance the day when hydrogen energy will become the principal means by which the world will achieve its long-sought goal of abundant clean energy for mankind. It stimulates the exchange of information in the hydrogen energy field through its publications and sponsorship of international workshops, short courses, and conferences. The association has an official scientific journal, *International Journal of Hydrogen Energy*, published monthly by Elsevier Science.

National Coal Association (NCA)
1130 Seventeenth St. NW, Washington, DC 20036
(202) 463-2653 • fax: (202) 833-1965

NCA is a national trade association that represents the coal industry. The association is primarily a lobbying organization that advocates the use of coal to meet America's energy needs. It publishes the weekly *Coal News* newsletter and the bimonthly magazine *Coal Voice*.

Natural Resources Defense Council (NRDC)
40 W. Twentieth St., New York, NY 10011
(212) 727-2700 • fax: (212) 727-1773
Web site: www.nrdc.org

The council is a nonprofit activist group composed of scientists, lawyers, and citizens who work to promote environmentally safe energy sources and protection of the environment. NRDC publishes a quarterly, *Amicus Journal*, the newsletter *Newsline*, and a bibliography of books concerning environmental issues.

Renewable Fuels Association (RFA)
1 Massachusetts Ave., Suite 820, Washington, DC 20001
(202) 289-3835 • fax: (202) 289-7519
Web site: www.ethanolrfa.org

The RFA is comprised of professionals who research, produce, and market renewable fuels, especially alcohol fuels. It also represents the renewable fuels industry before the federal government. RFA publishes the monthly newsletter *Ethanol Report.*

Union of Concerned Scientists (UCS)
2 Brattle Square, Cambridge, MA 02238-9105
(617) 547-5552 • fax: (617) 864-9405
Web site: www.ucsusa.org

UCS is an independent nonprofit alliance of more than one hundred thousand citizens and scientists concerned about nuclear energy and the impact of advanced technology on society. The organization conducts independent research, sponsors and participates in conferences, and testifies at congressional hearings. UCS publishes a quarterly newsletter, *Nucleus*, as well as books and reports.

World Nuclear Association (WNA)
114 Knightsbridge, Bowater House West, 12th Fl., London, England SW1X 7LJ
+44 (0) 20 7225 0303 • fax: +44 (0) 20 7225 0308
Web site: www.world-nuclear.org

The WNA is concerned with nuclear power generation and all aspects of the nuclear fuel cycle, including mining, conversion, enrichment, fuel fabrication, plant manufacture, transport, and the safe disposition of spent fuel. There are many resources available on its Web site, including a fifty-page essay titled *Why Tomorrow's World Needs Nuclear Energy.*

Bibliography

Books

Godfrey Boyle   *Renewable Energy*. New York: Oxford University Press, 2004.

Edward Cassedy   *Prospects for Sustainable Energy: A Critical Assessment*. New York: Cambridge University Press, 2000.

Julian Darley   *High Noon for Natural Gas: The New Energy Crisis*. White River Junction, VT: Chelsea Green, 2004.

Kenneth Deffeyes   *Hubbert's Peak: The Impending World Oil Shortage*. Princeton, NJ: Princeton University Press, 2003.

Bob Everett, Godfrey Boyle, and Janet Ramage   *Energy Systems and Sustainability*. New York: Oxford University Press, 2003.

Howard Geller   *Energy Revolution: Policies for a Sustainable Future*. Washington, DC: Island Press, 2003.

Richard Heinberg   *The Party's Over: Oil, War, and the Fate of Industrial Societies*. Gabriola, BC: New Society, 2003.

Jeremy Rifkin   *The Hydrogen Economy: The Creation of the World-Wide Energy Web and the Redistribution of Power on Earth*. New York: Jeremy P. Tarcher, 2002.

Paul Roberts   *The End of Oil: On the Edge of a Perilous New World*. New York: Houghton Mifflin, 2004.

Hermann Scheer   *The Solar Economy: Renewable Energy for a Sustainable Global Future*. London: Earthscan, 2004.

Periodicals

Mark Baard   "Hydrogen's Dirty Details," *Village Voice*, January 7–13, 2004.

Donald Barlett and James Steele   "The Oily Americans," *Time*, May 19, 2003.

John Carey   "With Oil over $50, Nukes Are Back," *Business Week*, November 8, 2004.

Rana Foroohar   "Eclipse of the Sun; Why Wall Street Investors Shun Renewable Energy," *Newsweek*, September 20, 2004.

David Freedman   "Fuel Cells vs. the Grid," *Technology Review*, January/February 2002.

Jeff Gerth	"Big Oil Steps Aside in Battle Over Arctic," *New York Times*, February 21, 2005.
Fred Guterl	"When Wells Go Dry," *Newsweek*, April 15, 2002.
David Johns	"Wilderness and Energy: The Battle Against Domination," *Wild Earth*, Fall 2002.
Nicola Jones and Bob Holmes	"Can Heavy Oil Avert an Energy Crisis?" *New Scientist*, August 2, 2003.
Amory Lovins	"How America Can Free Itself of Oil—Profitably," *Fortune*, October 2004.
John O'Dell	"Waving Yellow Flag on 'Green' Hybrid Vehicles," *Los Angeles Times*, March 7, 2004.
Peter Odell	"Oil Is Still King," *New Scientist*, November 6, 2004.
Paul Roberts	"Power Outage," *Los Angeles Times*, May 23, 2004.
Paul Roberts	"Running Out of Oil—and Time," *Los Angeles Times*, March 7, 2004.
Rebecca Smith	"Blackout Signals Major Weaknesses in U.S. Power Grid," *Wall Street Journal*, August 18, 2003.
Jonathan Tepperman	"Our Oil Policy Isn't Immoral," *Los Angeles Times*, April 29, 2004.
Nicholas Varchaver	"How to Kick the Oil Habit," *Fortune*, August 23, 2004.
Matthew L. Wald	"Wind Power Is Becoming a Better Bargain," *New York Times*, February 13, 2005.
J. Robinson West	"We Can't Get Along Without Saudi Oil," *Washington Post*, April 15–21, 2002.
Daniel Yergin	"Imagining a $7-a-Gallon Future," *New York Times*, April 4, 2004.

Index